EXPERIENTIAL MARKETING

EXPERIENTIAL MARKETING

SECRETS, STRATEGIES, AND SUCCESS STORIES FROM THE WORLD'S GREATEST BRANDS

KERRY SMITH
DAN HANOVER

FEATURING CASE STUDIES FROM
EVENT MARKETER MAGAZINE

WILEY

Library of Congress Cataloging-in-Publication Data
Names: Smith, Kerry, 1963- author. | Hanover, Dan, 1973- author.
Title: Experiential marketing : secrets, strategies, and success stories from
  the world's greatest brands / Kerry Smith, Dan Hanover.
Description: Hoboken, New Jersey : John Wiley & Sons, 2016. | Includes bibliographical
references and index.
Identifiers: LCCN 2015050877 | ISBN 9781119145875 (cloth) | ISBN 9781119145899
  (epub) | ISBN 9781119145882 (epdf)
Subjects: LCSH: Target marketing. | Branding (Marketing)
Classification: LCC HF5415.127 .S65 2016 | DDC 658.8--dc23 LC record available at
http://lccn.loc.gov/2015050877

Printed in the United States of America

10 9 8 7 6 5 4 3 2 1

For the brands that push the envelope—and the marketers who never settle.

Contents

Before We Begin

Your latest marketing campaign cost more than the last, yet reached half as many people.

Your celebrity endorsement deal has yet to generate any measurable returns.

Your online marketing campaign yielded no significant web traffic increase, and your brand's social media engagements declined.

You're being out-marketed by competitors who are spending a fraction of your budget, yet are capturing a larger share of the market.

What are you going to do?

Before you tell us, we're going to ask that you forget everything you know about marketing for a moment. Why you do it, how you were taught to use it, and what it accomplishes.

And then ask yourself one question: Are you open to a new approach—a way to break through the noise and connect with your target audience wherever they are, engage them in a way that generates tangible relationships, and convert them into customers?

If you are, then this book is for you.

Chapter One   The Rise of the Experience

Humans are social animals.

The need to gather and share stories dates back to the dawn of man, when our ancestors met around the fire to share in the kill and documented hunts on cave walls. Over thousands of years of political and social upheaval, natural and man-made disasters, and technological achievements that have shaped and reshaped our world, the need to share has remained constant—and it defines us as a species. But while our need to share stories has not changed over the millennia, the methods by which we share them have.

As a marketer, the need to cut through noise and tell *your* story has never been more important—or more difficult. In today's tune-out culture, where the interruptive marketing strategies of yesterday have been rendered almost useless by consumers who can now tune you out, brands need more than a catchy jingle, an amusing TV spot, or a big budget to be noticed. Being flashy, sexy, or loud no longer equates to a return on investment. Marketers have no one to blame but themselves for their current predicament. For decades, brands worshipped at the altar of mass reach—using GRPs, CPMs, and other quantitative metrics for delivering the most messages at the least cost, and in the

CPM – cost per view / GRP – gross rating point : impressions as a % of target pop process bombarding consumers with irrelevant messages at the wrong time. That approach doesn't create engagement; it creates exasperation. It's no wonder that, when given the opportunity to skip or block mass media, consumers do it in droves. And if traditional media clutter isn't challenging enough, today's customers are bypassing established media altogether and consuming content, sharing, and communicating via entirely new social and mobile platforms . . . which make them even harder to reach.

Brands have two choices: (1) continue to play cat-and-mouse with customers, trying to keep up with where they're going and adapting messaging to the medium du jour. We call this the "push" option, which requires you spend money to chase your consumers to their next favorite medium and then figure out how to interrupt them with your message. Or (2) take another path—one that taps into the core of our human DNA and virtually forces target audiences to stop, take notice, and participate. We call this the "pull" approach, and it is the central tenet of experiential marketing, a powerful strategy used more and more by leading brands to create true customer engagement that delivers measurable results.

In its simplest form, experiential marketing is nothing more than a highly evolved form of corporate storytelling. But while the premise appears simple—combine a brand message, elements of interactivity, a targeted audience, and deliver it in a live setting to create a defined outcome—successful experiences are both art and science. Embracing experiential marketing requires a new way of thinking about marketing, creativity, and the role of media in the overall mix.

This may sound a bit uncomfortable for many marketers, because it requires changing some very established ways of thinking and branding methods. But those who have transitioned to an experiential marketing mindset are finding that any pains of change are outweighed by the benefits of more powerful marketing, more engaged customers, and better returns on marketing investments.

This book is the culmination of more than a decade spent working with some of the biggest brands in the world, interviewing hundreds of marketers, and documenting thousands of experiential marketing programs. Throughout our years covering the leaders of the experiential marketing movement, we've isolated and identified key success factors that successful experience brands share. None began their journeys as highly evolved experiential marketers, but many can now claim expert status after years of trial and error. We are about to provide you with the collective insights and wisdom from the marketers who blazed the trail so you can proceed down this exciting new path.

THE EXPERIENCE R/EVOLUTION

There are four general pillars of all stories: The story, the storyteller, the medium by which the story is shared, and the listener. Eliminate any one of these and it's quite literally end-of-story.

Commercial storytelling took shape in the late 18th century as manufacturers shifted their focus from simply announcing the existence of their goods and services to using words and images that would persuade customers to buy theirs. Four factors ignited this movement toward "show and sell" corporate storytelling:

- The industrial revolution, which allowed manufacturers to generate products in mass quantities (and created pressure to stimulate mass consumption)
- An expanding transportation network that could take products to distant markets efficiently
- A growing media and retail infrastructure that could reach customers in virtually every market
- An exploding population with a voracious appetite for goods and services

Modern print advertising took off in the 1920s. Then radio lifted commercial messages off of printed pages and broadcast them into millions of living rooms. And newspapers began to work with "agencies" that called on companies to handle the process of selling, producing, and billing their ads. Over time, these agencies began understanding what made some ads more effective than others. They became advertising agencies.

After radio, of course, came television. It combined visuals with sound, and modern consumer marketing was born. But somewhere along the way, perhaps distracted by the glitz and glamour of Madison Avenue, brands lost sight of something fundamentally important. Marketing had become less about the story and the listener and all about the storyteller and the medium. Companies outbid each other for primetime placement of messages; they bought print ads via computer programs based on demographics; they escalated the arms race of spending in order to proclaim dominance; and they became servants to the media that carried their messages. (Years ago we asked a creative director at one of the biggest ad agencies whether he ever saw a marketing challenge that couldn't be solved with a 30-second TV spot. He couldn't think of one.)

It was a time when the loudest voice garnered the biggest market share. And bigger budgets begat louder voices. But economic turmoil has a way of shaking up the status quo. The first real crack in the wall happened during the Savings and Loan Crisis in 1989, which put the country into an 18-month-long recession that ended in March 1991. The tumult jolted marketers into trying to find ways to boost sales, and it was during this period that it became clear that the two beliefs upon which marketing was based—that if people are aware they will buy and that the definition of success is reaching the most people—were both false.

This coincided with the collapse of the Soviet Union during the same year when, less than a month after Lenin's statue was pulled down, a regional root beer brand in New Orleans with a miniscule marketing budget was looking for a way to boost sales over the summer. Barq's announced it was having a "Soviet Union Going Out of Business Sale." The brand dispatched one of its marketers to Russia with $70,000 in his pocket, which he used to fill a shipping container with two tons of Metrushka dolls, Lenin Day pins, tank commander watches, and military medals, all of which were to be offered in a promotion that gave consumers a Soviet tchotchke in exchange for proof-of-purchase from a 12-pack of Barq's root beer. It ignited the age of promotion marketing. The creative stunt received worldwide press, nearly 100 percent bottler participation, and a 30 percent bump in sales (the brand was ultimately acquired by The Coca-Cola Co.). The thinking of the day was that advertising could change people's minds, but promotion could change their behavior.

For a decade after Barq's reminded marketers that a great story could trump a big budget, this type of promotion marketing thrived as marketers discovered that combining compelling stories with purchase incentives could help gain distribution, sell product, and combat competitive activity. During this time, the ad agency conglomerates shifted from buying each other in the mid-1980s to buying promotion agencies in the mid-1990s, combining their core creative and media buying capabilities with so-called "below-the-line" promotion services to offer clients a full suite of marketing support.

Supporting the rise of promotion marketing was a study issued at the time by an industry trade group representing retail display manufacturers that found two-thirds of all purchasing decisions were made in the store. So for all the money that marketers had been pouring into traditional advertising, consumers were making their purchase decisions within feet of checkout lanes. The findings provided support for those who were espousing the benefits of combining a brand message with an incentive to drive action and building a compelling story around the effort to create excitement.

It was the first step in the experiential marketing movement.

The marketing mix continued to expand. Advertising and promotion were joined by in-store marketing, direct marketing, and later online marketing. At most companies, each "marketing silo," as they were called, was developed on its own and operated independently. As a result, the marketing mix evolved as pieces, not as a collective, which is why until the mid-1990s, marketing portfolios were largely a collection of separate tools, rather than parts of a single engine that worked together. Each was funded independently and often managed by dedicated teams—the direct marketing department, the online marketing team, the advertising group, and so on. They each had independent goals, different brand standards, even different compensation incentives that varied from group to group. In some cases, the different teams worked together on campaigns—most times they did not. The lack of internal coordination or strategy for integrating marketing or at least aligning around common business goals created turf battles, conflicting messaging, and enough other inefficiencies and confusion to mask the weaknesses of current marketing and the larger potential of using an experiential strategy. (Many companies today are still set up this way, but their numbers are dwindling as financial pressures have forced marketing departments to operate more efficiently.)

Throughout it all, marketers had been dabbling "off the grid" with something called "branded events."

- The Pepsi Challenge served blind sips of soda to consumers and essentially turned millions of consumers into an army of branded spokespeople.
- Toy giant Saban launched a weekend Power Rangers family tour that turned 31 Walmarts into kid-friendly festivals. More than 4,000 fans attended each—sales increased by 400 percent.
- American Express staged a free Sheryl Crow concert in New York City's Central Park to promote a new Blue credit card aimed at younger shoppers. The event aired via the first-ever national "trimulcast" on Fox TV stations, 60 radio stations, and blueconcerts.com. A "Blue Crew" distributed 25,000 concert tickets around New York City to drive card applications. The number of cards in force exceeded goals by 71 percent and applications by 150 percent.
- To increase sales of its Tamiflu medication, Roche sent glass-enclosed ("germ-free") residences built on the backs of flatbed trucks into 70 cities. Each was home to an actor conducting his daily activities (sleeping, eating, working on the computer), seemingly oblivious to the commotion he caused outside his walls. The punch line was displayed on all sides of the vehicles: "One person in this town who can probably feel safe from the flu. For the rest of us flu sufferers, there's Tamiflu." Tamiflu outsold its competitor by a three-to-one margin and gained a 58 percent share of market.

But as successful as these campaigns were, most suffered from a lack of support, funding, and understanding—the programs were considered one-shots . . . or advertising spinoffs, as many called them. Brave marketers continued to experiment with live events to reach and engage customers who were becoming increasingly difficult to reach using traditional methods. Incremental successes bred repeated programs and a growing legion of live marketing believers. Yet marketers were telling us that without credible information—best practices, case studies, research—they were having a difficult time convincing management to approve "real" expenditures on larger-scale experiential initiatives.

Our own journey began around that time. We noticed an incredible number of major brands moving marketing budgets out of traditional media and redeploying them into face-to-face channels where they could get closer to their customers in the hopes of boosting sales. Our friends Joe Pine and Jim Gilmore were about to publish *The Experience Economy* (1999), in which they predicted that future economic growth lay in the value of experiences. Touting the merits of goods and services was no longer enough; brands were on the threshold of a new economic era in which all businesses would orchestrate memorable experiences to win customers.

RECALIBRATING THE MARKETING MIX

By the end of 1999, amid TiVo, Google, and satellite radio, it became clear that what had worked relatively well for 50 years was showing its age. Clutter was everywhere, and marketing campaigns powered by separate silos were fragmented, stepping on each other, and screaming too many things at too many people. Put another way, the different parts of the marketing mix started competing with, rather than complementing, each other.

In an effort to recalibrate the marketing mix and begin to generate more unified, programmatic campaigns, brands such as IBM, Samsung, General Electric, and Microsoft began hiring CMOs to combine their separate marketing silos, spends, and teams into a singular marketing function—reasoning that the sum of the parts would work more effectively than the independent pieces.

They called it "integrated marketing."

But little did marketers know that combining the separate channels to leverage individual strengths would also expose weaknesses hidden for decades. We'll get to that in a minute.

Meanwhile, what had been a small subsection of marketers testing live branded events began to grow. When Bell Atlantic became Verizon, the company tried a novel strategy for connecting consumers to the new brand. The brand installed temporary luge tracks at six ski resorts. Consumers could suit up and fly down for practice runs in the morning; in the afternoon, brave participants were split into age/gender groups for competitions. The entire time, teams from Verizon were on hand to explain the new brand, hand out information, answer questions—and above all else, have a conversation. "You have to be there to see it. People are going crazy for it," Verizon director of corporate sponsorships Pat Hennebry told us in 1999. "We're giving them something they would never get to experience on their own and no ad could provide."

One by one, other companies followed. When Lincoln signed a then-historic five-year, $20 million U.S. Open tennis sponsorship, the carmaker went beyond standard sports signage and ticket packages by converting an unused building at the USTA Tennis Center in New York City into an interactive Lincoln American Luxury Immersion. The structure's interior featured soundstages, faux docks with real water, and images of tennis through the decades. Some 30,000 leads were collected from visitors strolling through the structure. "It's something very new for the consumer to be able to interact with a brand this way," Andrea Memenas, Lincoln's head of marketing communications, told us in 2000. "This new type of marketing is starting to permeate our entire marketing mix."

More and more, brands got in on the action. Anheuser-Busch unveiled a multi-million-dollar Bud World road show, billed as "the ultimate Budweiser experience," that unfurled from a 53-foot tractor trailer that was part school, part museum, and part Hollywood extravaganza. It toured 120 cities and attracted 130,000 consumers with three "experiences." In the "World of Budweiser," guests took an historical tour of the beer maker's 136-year history. A "BudVision" theater, complete with stadium seating and widescreen booming surround-sound effects, took them on a sensory ride through the brand's vast consumer reach, from hop fields in Idaho to NASCAR races. Guests then headed to the "Bud Brew House," where Anheuser-Busch brewmasters taught them about the brewing process. Visitors touched and smelled ingredients, discussed a variety of topics, tasted (where legal) the frosty stuff, and received personalized "Certified Beer Master" wallet cards. "We're trying to create more than an impression," Karen Branding, A-B's vice president, told us in 2000. "We're trying to create a memory."

Despite the increased activities, these types of experiential campaigns were given a variety of labels—alternative marketing, branded events, non-traditional marketing, grassroots marketing, presence marketing, lifestyle marketing, and so on. But those labels failed to properly define the programs and made it difficult to see that a new marketing discipline was forming.

At the same time, that act of integrating the separate pieces of the marketing mix provided newly installed CMOs with the first accurate portrait of their company's marketing performance. Ever. Finally, these new heads of marketing around the world could watch, manage, and measure their marketing functions as a single engine after five decades of the pieces operating independently.

Enter *Event Marketer* magazine, which we launched in 2002 to serve the information needs of corporate marketing executives hungry for information they could use to make their campaigns more effective and to sell-in programs to management. Our mission was not just to provide information to practitioners, but to facilitate the formation of an experiential industry—one that would be seen not as a part of some other marketing discipline, but as a discipline in and of itself.

At an industry conference in 2003, Coca-Cola Co. chief operating officer Steve Heyer stood before a room of marketers from the biggest brands in the world and proclaimed in a keynote heard around the world: "We're thinking about marketing in a radically different way. And I'd suggest that those of you here today who aren't yet thinking this way ought to start right now. Economic and social developments demand a new approach to connecting with consumers."

He noted seven factors that were changing the marketing paradigm:

- The economic landscape around media cost-efficiencies
- The escalation of marketing costs
- The trifecta of media fragmentation, media ownership consolidation, and wholesale unbundling

- The erosion of mass markets
- The empowerment of consumers who "have an unrivaled ability to edit and avoid advertising"
- A consumer trend toward mass customization and personalization
- And last but not least, those seven little words that would trigger a global marketing revolution: "The emergence of an experience-based economy."

"Corporate marketers will [no longer] reflexively turn to TV advertising when what we [want] is powerful communications and consumer connections," he said. "We're moving to ideas that elicit emotion and create connections. Do we need reach and frequency? No. We need connections with our targets."

We were there. You could have heard a pin drop. "Experience-based, access-driven marketing is our next frontier." He called marketers still buying reach and frequency "lost," and said the new marketing mix had to be used to "create an ever-expanding variety of interactions for people that—over time—build a relationship."

The use of live experiences began to accelerate. Pepsi-Cola Co.'s Fruit Works invaded Spring Break with a "Free Ride" bus cruising busy strips picking up and dropping off party-minded college kids (who often can't rent cars because of their age) at clubs and hotels. Passengers received free drinks, played games for prizes, rocked to music, and had their pictures taken—back at school, they could access the photos and e-mail them to friends. "We were interacting with consumers exactly where *they* interacted," Robin Kaminsky, Pepsi's director of alternative beverages, told us. "Experiential marketing is about showing customers that your brand wants to be a part of their lives."

Unilever's Slim-Fast turned New Year's resolutions into reality with one-day Slim-Fast Challenge events inside 3,500 Walmart stores that had consumers signing up for a 12-week program, meeting with dieticians, and purchasing three months' worth of product. Elsewhere, Levi's deployed a 10-city Style@Work program, where stylists invaded white-collar districts to offer fashion tips and wardrobe makeovers. Sales jumped 30 percent in each market visited.

By 2010, Heyer's predictions had become a reality. Product by product and brand by brand, the consumer had assumed control of every marketing channel—limiting reach, changing functionality, and dictating effectiveness. The balance of power shifted from brands to their customers. And the marketing blueprint used for decades by companies such as McDonald's, AT&T, Nike, and Kraft was in need of significant triage.

- *Advertising.* Above-the-line advertising was changed forever by the onset of satellite radio and the DVR. For the first time ever, consumers could opt out of advertising—a decision, it turns out, they'd never reverse. Upwards of 85 percent of consumers skip commercials today.
- *Promotion.* Customers became so accustomed to discounts that many wouldn't buy without one. The average discount used to "incent" shoppers grew so large that some companies compensated with top-line price increases, forever compromising the original premise of promotion (a small discount to drive a purchase). Today, 20 percent is the average discount used to generate a measurable swing in unaided purchase intent, up from 5 percent two decades ago.
- *Direct Marketing.* Printing and postage costs surged over the years. Changing direct mail rules and regulations added extra logistics and even more costs. Rising consciousness of eco-friendliness put pressure on brands to use recycled materials. And the ability to reach consumers where they lived and worked was eventually overshadowed by the realization that they were literally labeling direct mail as junk. More than 55 percent of all direct mail is thrown away.
- *e-Mail Marketing.* The proliferation of spam filters and server guards sent e-mail click-through rates plummeting to around 3 percent as customers began to block unsolicited e-mails. Any marketer celebrating a 3 percent open-rate success should really be lamenting a 97 percent failure.
- *Online Advertising.* What for years offered unprecedented reach, pay-per-click affordability, and the most measureable form of marketing in history, was struck down by pop-up blockers, ad tracking limiters,

cache wipers, and the ability to simply turn off cookies in web and mobile browser preferences—yet another marketing channel that customers had the power to turn off.

- *Social Media.* Marketers relished the ability to attract unlimited "followers" who "like" their brands, using their social media pages as platforms for creating dialogs like their corporate homepages never could. But getting somebody to like a brand turned out to be much easier than getting them to love one—or even use or purchase it. Studies show that only 3 to 6 percent of a brand's social media followers actually engage them. And a large percentage of social followers eventually "unfollow" a brand.

Throughout it all, a new discipline was evolving. From HP, Intel, Adidas, and 7-Up to Kraft, Nissan, Rolex, and Target, companies embraced experiential marketing as the new mainstream, initially funding live events out of ineffective above-the-line marketing budgets. *Mobile marketing tours, sponsorships, pop-up stores.* What was once something a few brands were testing became something a lot of brands were using, and many even created dedicated experiential marketing departments and teams. *Trade shows, proprietary events, street marketing.* The same programs that had been mere advertising add-ons quickly became the campaigns that advertising was being added onto. *Mall marketing, nightlife events, PR events, road shows.* And experiential programs once considered unmeasurable were returning some of the best ROI spikes in decades. *Sales meetings, sampling tours, guerrilla marketing, in-store experiences.*

Today, what was long labeled "non-traditional" marketing has become the new traditional. And it has a name: Experiential Marketing.

Virtually every major brand on the planet has adopted an experiential marketing channel into its marketing mix, and many of them have positioned experiential as the lead discipline—with advertising, online, direct, and the rest of the mix playing supporting roles behind live events. Globally, more than $100 billion (USD) is spent annually on experiential programs by tens of thousands of companies. It is the fastest-growing form of marketing in the history of, well, *marketing.*

People frequently ask us why experiential marketing grew so quickly, almost out of nowhere, and why so many companies use it. We don't have a single answer. We have seven:

- *It Carries the Strength of Many*. Experiential marketing allows marketers to combine the best parts of the marketing mix into a single channel—leaving behind each silo's weaknesses. The best experiential programs benefit from the impact of advertising without wasted reach; the motivation of promotion without a deep discount; the targetability of direct marketing without the junk mail reflex; the mass connectivity of social media but with real engagement; and so on. Like a great chef can combine unique ingredients to make a stunning dish, experiential marketing takes the best qualities of the marketing mix and accomplishes in a single channel what for 50 years required six. Webster defines a mutation as: "a change in the genes . . . that causes physical characteristics that are different from what is considered normal; a new form of something that has changed." Often we refer to experiential marketing as a mutated marketing mix—an evolved form of a blueprint that needed added strength and resilience.
- *It's Unstoppable*. Experiential marketing represents the last marketing channel customers don't have complete control over. They can skip commercials and block ads. They can toss mail, tag e-mails as spam, and unlike a Facebook page. But the face-to-face connection is undeniable, unbreakable—and unblockable. There is no live DVR. The human connection cannot be tuned out. In an age of customer-controlled tune-out, experiential marketing represents that last "pure" marketing medium for brand-to-customer dialogs.
- *It's the First Singular Converter*. Gone are the days when marketers used different marketing channels (and budgets) to push consumers through the purchase funnel. Advertising was used for the awareness stage, promotion used for the consideration stage, and so on. What we've learned is that experiential marketing gives brands the ability to stop connecting disparate disciplines and instead use a single marketing channel. When used correctly, experiential marketing can turn prospects into aware customers who understand the product, have interest in buying it, and actually make purchases.

- *It's an Accelerant.* Experiential marketing can affect how quickly customers move through the purchase funnel. When we've compared a traditional multi-silo marketing campaign to an experiential program, we see that more often than not, experiential marketing converts consumers into customers faster than any other form of marketing.
- *It Drives Lifetime Value.* Live experiences are hard to forget—and that's the point. Experiential marketing creates a more immediate bond with consumers and generates a more substantive relationship with them. Relationships, as we'll discuss in Chapter 2, form the building blocks of brand loyalty, which dictates purchase frequency.
- *It's an Engagement Multiplier.* Experiential marketing flips the passive model of traditional marketing into an interactive platform on which brands have actual conversations with customers and can put actual products in their hands. Consumers are more engaged with brands during experiences. They share their experiences with more people. Preference and intent spike. Brand affinity rises.
- *It's the Marketing Mix's Charger.* One of the biggest benefits of experiential marketing is the impact it has on the rest of the marketing mix. Integrated campaigns that lead with experiences are seeing the other marketing pillars actually benefit from the alignment. Ad recall, website traffic, social media connections, incentive redemption—all show remarkable increases when connected to experiential marketing strategy. And the live event has emerged as an incredible feeder of content . . . *for the rest of the marketing mix.* Trade show booths are serving as recording studios for YouTube videos. General session keynotes at business-to-business events are being captured and redistributed as investor briefings, sales overviews, and employee messages. Bud Light's 2015 Super Bowl TV spots were filmed entirely at its events.

THE NEW BRANDING FRONTIER

Does experiential marketing represent an evolution or a revolution? Both. Live experiences have ignited a marketing revolution in which brands around the world have committed to upgrading their marketing strategies, budgets, and platforms. And that revolution has driven a much-needed evolution of the marketing channels and silos used by brands for more than 50 years. Use of experiential marketing has exploded as more marketers invest in building programs that create true customer engagement and real business results.

We have been chronicling this evolution for over a decade, and along the way we built the world's largest portfolio of content and community around the subject of experiential marketing, including our Experiential Marketing Summit, the world's largest annual gathering of experiential marketing professionals; our Ex Awards, the preeminent recognition program for experiential campaigns; our Event Marketing Institute, from which we conduct research and provide business training; and *Event Marketer* and its website, which provide more than a million marketers each year with content. We have consulted and trained hundreds of the world's largest brands on experiential marketing trends and hosted more than 10,000 of their marketers at our training events.

It's from this perspective that we've written *Experiential Marketing*, to provide a roadmap for those who are considering transitioning to an experiential strategy—and for those already well along the path, to prepare you for what's next.

REFERENCE

Pine, B.J., & Gilmore, J.H. (1998). *The experience economy*. Boston, MA: Harvard Business School Press.

Chapter Two   The Psychology of Engagement

James Comer said that no significant learning can occur without a significant relationship.

For decades, just three differentiators—or as we call them, core value propositions (CVPs)—distinguished brands from one another and drove all marketing campaigns: price, performance, and service.

From HP and Ford to Procter & Gamble and Cisco, marketing decisions and campaigns were made and deployed based on creating alignment, perception, and affinity around those three CVPs. Most marketing campaigns traditionally lead with a single CVP, using price (Walmart) or performance (Intel) or service (Zappos) as the primary differentiators— the main "reason" for customers to buy. But some companies (JetBlue) promoted all three CVPs in an effort to communicate a stronger position that provided customers with low pricing, high performance, and premium service. Others (Toyota, Verizon, Lowe's) rotated the lead CVP across different marketing programs or times of the year.

But over the years, heightened competition and fragmentation eventually commoditized the three CVP drivers. In nearly every category, virtually every brand began to promote lower prices, high performance, and excellent service. Put another way, the marketing campaigns and the brand promises became nearly identical. The logos and taglines may have been different, but the messaging was the same.

It all begged the question: If marketers were no longer differentiating their brands, why were people choosing to buy them?

Because, as it turned out, there weren't three core value propositions— *there were four.* Yes, purchase decisions had been primarily influenced by price, performance, and service. But we found that purchases, more and more, were actually being driven by a fourth CVP: relationship.

Studies, focus groups, and market research began to show that consumers who considered themselves to be "in a relationship" with a company were less influenced by price, performance, and service. As a result, they remained incredibly loyal—less because of cost, product features, or service, and more because of the loyalty that being in a relationship generated. Hence, marketers around the world began to embrace relationship marketing, which provided the promise (and premise) that those brands that could develop and keep a relationship could develop and keep their customers. Forever.

Our own surveys of more than 5,000 consumers spanning 10 years found that the majority of customers who consider themselves to have a relationship with a company or brand pointed to the intersection (Figure 2.1) of four Brand Relationship Drivers:

- *Driver 1.* They identified with the brand.
- *Driver 2.* The brand helped them or solved a problem.
- *Driver 3.* The brand had specific meaning to them.
- *Driver 4.* They felt better about themselves when they used the brand.

With the long-term benefits a relationship provided to brands came a transfer of power from companies to their customers. Gone were the days of using one-way marketing to stimulate sales. A relationship, by definition, requires two active and willing participants who show intent to each other. Without relationship *intent,* there can be no relationship *consent.* And while brands can't create relationship intent for the customer, they can foster, accelerate, and influence it—with experiences.

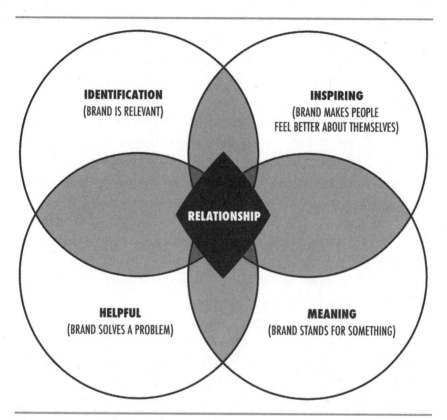

FIGURE 2.1   Relationship Intersection

Successfully creating and using experiences to generate long-term relationships requires an understanding of how an experience scientifically fosters a relationship. Noted behavioral experts and psychologists agree that the human mind computes experiences in specific ways—and the brain processes more information in a single day than any supercomputer does in a year. If marketers understand how the mind processes information and emotions, they can create more relevant experiences and, more importantly, deliberately construct engagements around a specific behavioral outcome.

THE SCIENCE BEHIND RELATIONSHIPS

Experiences create emotions that drive people to respond to each other and "feel" a certain way. According to Jonathan Turner (Turner & Stets, 2005), an emotion technically emerges as the brain connects neurotransmitters, neuroactive peptides, and hormones—resulting in the musculoskeletal system generating a mental and emotional response. When we have a feeling, it's the neocortex being stimulated by neuropathways. The temporal lobes process sound, music, face, and object recognition. The occipital lobes process what is seen. And the parietal lobes manage spatial reasoning (Sousa, 2011).

Although it wasn't until the 1970s that behavioral psychologists and sociologists began to study emotions as a collective, some research dates back to the early 1900s. In 1912, French sociologist Émile Durkheim published his studies of Aboriginal gatherings in Central Australia, finding that when groups of Aboriginals came together, levels of excitement increased, and a kind of "collective effervescence emerged" (Durkheim, 1995, p. 117). It was the first sociological project of its kind. Durkheim specifically noted that emotions were stimulated and generated during the course of a face-to-face interaction.

Some 50 years later, Canadian-born sociologist and writer Erving Goffman, a self-proclaimed disciple of Durkheim, analyzed and expanded on Durkheim's work (Goffman, 1961). Goffman found that deeper "encounters" took place within gatherings. He was ahead of his time, as sociologists would later reclassify encounters as experiences. He said that these encounters were composed of five elements:

1. A single visual and cognitive focus of attention
2. A mutual openness to verbal communication
3. An eye-to-eye huddle
4. A feeling of togetherness
5. Ceremonial openings, closings, entrances, and exits

Marketers use experiences to affect a target audience. No matter the audience or the company, there is always the intention to use an experience to distribute a message or content that incites an emotion or action (a behavioral response). Sociologists David Perkins and Gabriel Salomon (1992, p. 2) refer to this as transfer: "Transfer is the ability to take what one has learned in one context and use it in a new instance."

There are two parts to effective Experience Transfer (Figure 2.2):

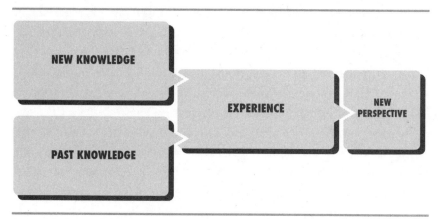

FIGURE 2.2   Experience Transfer

1. *Part 1. Transfer During Learning.* The act of providing content and messaging to a target audience.
2. *Part 2. Transfer of Learning.* When a target audience absorbs the new learning into what they already know and leave an experience with a new perspective and knowledge base on a subject or topic (or company).

Perkins and Salomon reminded marketers that not all transfer was good, and in fact wrote extensive papers outlining the specific differences between positive transfer (when learning benefits the learner) and negative transfer (when learning conflicts or confuses the learner). Obviously, these are just a few insights into the emotional and behavioral impact an experience makes on a target audience. But there are four takeaways for marketers:

1. You should design experiences that provoke transfer. How people feel about something impacts their interest in it, their devoted attention, and their desire to interact and store information.
2. Engagement is more likely to be processed, stored, and remembered if the engagement uses meaning and relevance to strike a chord or emotion. When we ask if something makes sense, we're asking whether it has meaning—and we define meaning as something that

fits into a learner's past experiences. When we ask whether something is engaging, we're analyzing the relevance—and we define relevance as a topic or situation that is both needed and wanted.

3. If you understand that emotions affect attention and learning, you can design experiences that specifically evoke a certain emotion or behavior. Although experiential marketing (Figure 2.3) uses the five senses to bring a brand to life, target audiences do not use all five senses equally. People have learning preferences and default to one or two senses over the others. We call these specific learning channels a person's "learning profile." Psychologist and psychometrician Robert Sternberg's Triarchic Theory of Intelligence (1988) studied three patterns of intelligence learners: analytical, creative, and practical.

   ○ Analytical learners evaluate and critique information as they receive it and make a judgment to embrace it or deny it. *Is this relevant for me?*

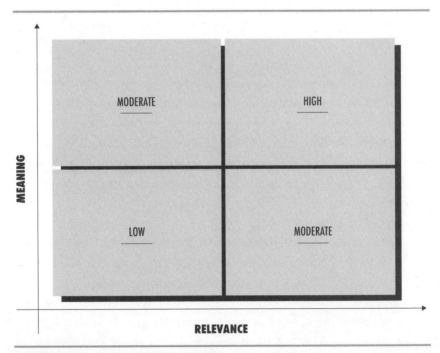

FIGURE 2.3   Experiential Recall

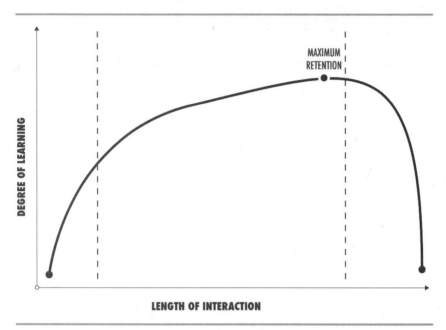

FIGURE 2.4   Experience Retention

- Creative learners convert information into ideas and inspiration for current or future solutions. *How will I use this?*
- Practical learners accept information as content they'll use and apply. *I know how I will use this.*

4. Understanding how a person learns should dictate how a company is providing information to them within an experience. Experiences generate what is called a working memory, essentially a temporary memory that may or may not be converted into a permanent one. Experts agree that longer experiences greatly increase the chances of long-term memory association between an audience and a brand (Figure 2.4).

Interaction is key to avoiding low-value temporary memory and ensuring permanent resonance. Experiences leverage two types of interactions (Sousa, 2011):

- *Intrinsic Interactions.* Activities and engagements with high connection to a target's needs, values, interests, and attitudes.

   ◦ *Extrinsic Interactions.* Interactions the target is motivated to participate in, via encouragement from peers or rewards/awards.

Put another way, any experience can generate short-term memory. But only the significant ones are converted into long-term stored memories—often called "long-term potentiation" (LTP).

LEARNING DRIVES UNDERSTANDING

George Washington Carver proclaimed that all learning is understanding relationships. Recognizing that there is science behind the idea that relevant experiences foster stronger relationships and stimulate greater message retention should encourage marketers to ensure that their experiential strategies are being designed and choreographed to engage both the heart—and the mind.

REFERENCES

Durkheim, É. (1995). *The elementary forms of religious life*. New York: The Free Press.

Goffman, E. (1961). *Encounters: Two studies in the sociology of instruction*. Eastford, CT: Martino Fine Books.

Perkins, D., & Salomon, G. (1992). *Instructional encyclopedia of education* (2nd ed.). Oxford, UK: Pergamon Press.

Sousa, D.A. (2011). *How the brain learns* (4th ed.). Thousand Oaks, CA: Corwin.

Sternberg, R. (1988). *The triarchic mind: A new theory of intelligence*. New York: Viking Press.

Turner, J.H., & Stets, J.E. (2012). *The sociology of emotions*. New York: Cambridge University Press.

Chapter Three   Developing an Experiential Strategy

Across all categories of products and services, experiential marketing is used in different ways—and for different reasons.

Some brands use experiences to recruit new customers, while others use live engagements for retention. Many companies use experiential marketing for generating trial, while others use the discipline for generating PR. From changing perception to changing sales pipelines, from in-store engagements at retail to guerrilla experiences on street corners—pop-up stores and sales meetings, media launches and developer conferences—the brand experience has become the marketer's most fluid engagement tool. It can be used in multiple ways for multiple reasons and is considered the modern brand manager's ultimate utility player. (One Fortune 10 CMO once told us that he considered experiential marketing a sort of Swiss Army Knife for brands.)

But as flexible as it is, and as the many ways marketers use it multiply, the most effective experiential marketing strategies have several shared traits. We've studied more than 10,000 experiential campaigns over the last decade and have found successful experience strategies are grounded in five Core Experience Strategy Platforms. (We often refer to these as The Big C's.)

CONNECTION

At the heart of every experiential marketing strategy is the goal of creating a "connection" with an audience, as a conduit for inciting an action and developing a relationship.

But not all brands need to create the same kind of connection. Some need to create an information-anchored connection, others a more emotional-driven one. Savvy marketers understand first what kind of connections they need to make, and they build their experiential strategies around them. There are eight Experience Connection types:

- *Emotional Connections.* An experiential program used to elicit an emotional response from the target. We often say when we're training a marketing department that if a brand can bring somebody to tears, they have accomplished what few have. Experiences have the power to move people. From community events and cause marketing to unique programs that unite audiences, demographics, even towns and cities, Emotional Connections allow brands to transcend traditional marketing channels that merely appeal to the eyes, and instead use experiences to affect the heart.

  Example: To leverage its position as a key stakeholder within NASCAR's efforts to benefit Nationwide Children's Hospital (NCH), Nationwide Insurance created the inaugural Nationwide Children's Hospital 200, the first NASCAR Nationwide Series race at Mid-Ohio Sports Car Course in Lexington, Ohio. A promotional event took place before the race during which hospital patients had the opportunity to race pinewood derby cars against NASCAR drivers Austin Dillon and Brian Scott.

  A "Patient Champion" program was created for the event to honor current and former patients at the hospital. Children were identified, matched with NASCAR Nationwide Series teams and drivers, and treated as VIPs during the race. Ten Patient Champions and their families participated in memorable, unique experiences on race day, including welcoming the drivers at a Driver's Meeting and being honored by all attendees; being introduced as VIP guests and accompanying their paired drivers across a Driver Introductions stage; leading the crowd in the Pledge of Allegiance; and giving the "Drivers, Start Your Engines" command as shown on the national race broadcast.

Driver Alex Bowman, whose car bore an NCH paint scheme with a Patient Champion on the hood, visited a mobile display to help fans learn about donation opportunities. A Nationwide Children's Hospital Monarch 1 helicopter provided a flyover at the conclusion of the National Anthem and remained on display at the track.

- *Educational Connections.* The use of information as the primary connection driver. Most often used by business-to-business brands to inform internal employees as well as external prospects and clients about new products, service usage, and company changes. Business-to-consumer companies also use Educational Connections, to teach consumers about a brand, product, or category. Our own research shows that if a customer understands a product, he or she is four times more likely to buy it.

Example: Oculus may be all about virtual reality, but its first developer conference had two very real goals in mind—to keep those developing Oculus-compatible content and technology in the loop with upcoming Oculus technology and to excite developers about new products. It delivered on both counts. To attract current and potential developers, the conference featured keynote speeches, workshops, and demo opportunities.

Oculus CEO Brendan Iribe and other prominent Oculus executives led the keynotes and discussed the future of Oculus technology as well as the field of virtual reality as a whole, reinforcing Oculus's position as the industry leader. Attendees were encouraged to bring the technology, games, and other virtual reality experiences they had developed for the Oculus platform. They could share their products and receive feedback from Oculus team members in designated demonstration areas. The combination of speeches and presentations by industry leaders, along with workshops and demo stations, allowed for more personal, hands-on sessions without sacrificing the efficiency of larger presentations.

By blending together elements of conferences, conventions, and VIP events, the Oculus Connect event defied labels. Attendees showed off their equipment without having to pay for booth space as they would at traditional shows. And while attendees at most business conferences are passive consumers of the content being presented, developers at this event had the opportunity to shape the experience and contribute to the content. This mirrored Oculus's own objective: to encourage developers to keep contributing to Oculus-compatible content.

- *Surprise and Delight Connections.* Seemingly random but completely designed and choreographed connections that use the act of surprising someone as a catalyst for connecting with them. Our own studies show that a surprise experience causes spikes in memory and a lasting impact that far exceeds traditional marketing recall numbers.

Example: With so many products in the premium bottled water category, Evian needed to regain market share and relevance among consumers. It also had a new bottle design to launch. What better month of the year to get satisfying cold water into the hands of consumers than during August, one of the hottest in the United States? Knowing its Millennial target wouldn't respond to overt marketing ploys, Evian decided to put a cheeky twist on "premium" bottled water.

Over two days, the brand hit New York City's Madison Square Park, Union Square, Washington Square Park, and Bryant Park. Consumers within these areas were encouraged via Evian's social media channels to tweet to @evianwater using #evianBottleService to request a delivery. Once a tweet was received, the community management team responded to arrange a delivery. Within minutes, brand ambassadors were dispatched on custom Evian-branded bicycles to that person's location.

One brand ambassador presented the bottle of Evian on a silver tray while a second ambassador opened an umbrella, offering the individual a few moments of shade from the summer sun. To help drive buzz, Evian partnered with tennis star Maria Sharapova, the brand's global ambassador, to help kick off the campaign by delivering bottle service to one lucky consumer. As a result of the integrated effort, Evian drove a 5.2 percent increase in New York sales year over year.

- *Intercept Connections.* Experiences designed to take place on street corners, malls, subway stations, airports, and Main Streets. Often labeled as street or guerrilla marketing. Some brands subscribe to the notion that the busier the location, the more connections they'll generate. Others believe that the more obscure the intercept destination, the more memorable the connection. We've seen enough examples to know that both schools of thought produce calibrated and appropriate connectivity.

Examples: To increase traffic to retail locations in key markets during the holiday shopping season, The North Face, purveyor of technically advanced outdoor products and apparel, staged flash mob–style snowball fights with a twist.

Brand ambassadors outfitted in The North Face apparel engaged with each other on streets surrounding each location. Consumers who stopped to gawk at the action were handed mock snowballs made of foam that contained instructions to go to the nearby store to "unlock the duffel." The ball featured a QR code that displayed the campaign's rules.

When snowball-wielding consumers arrived at the store, they were directed to a table with a box full of keys and a locked North Face duffle bag full of gift cards. Each consumer could select one key from the box and try to unlock the duffle. Those who succeeded took away gift cards worth $25, $50, or $100. (In total, 275 were given away.) Those who didn't win still received a 10 percent off coupon for taking part in the event. More than 22,400 consumers participated.

Elsewhere, to generate buzz for the premiere of its new scripted series "Girlfriend's Guide to Divorce," about a self-help author dealing with an impending divorce, Bravo queued up stunts on the streets of Los Angeles and New York City that made heads turn and fingers post to social. The first stunt played off the show's main character's experience with a younger man.

Bravo unleashed 35 shirtless male models on Rodeo Drive and Santa Monica Promenade in Los Angeles wearing positive, painted messages on their chests. The second stunt started with a video Bravo created of a woman exacting revenge on her ex's Porsche—all "caught" on tape in the unlucky guy's driveway. Security footage showed the scorned lover armed with eggs and spray paint, scrawling phrases like "We Are Over" on the vehicle.

The video was seeded on YouTube and Reddit under anonymous accounts, and overnight thousands of people watched and shared the video. Bravo then took that story to the streets of New York City with three branded tow trucks that paraded the destroyed ex-lovers' cars, including the Porsche, which literally stopped traffic. The social sphere boomed with hashtag #GG2D as people posted photos and hypothesized on what the exes had done, until they realized it was a stunt for an upcoming show. The stunt generated 27.4 million impressions, and 100 percent of surveyed onlookers taking a photo with their phone confirmed they were posting to social media sites.

- *Influencer Connections.* Engaging a smaller group of people with an experience designed to trigger a connection with a larger pool of targets. Typically involves contact with targeted influencers, who then share their experience with friends and family, essentially serving as a surrogate connection generator and amplifier. Use of Influencer Connections grew exponentially once social media channels became viable amplification platforms (it became that much easier and affordable to target influencers who consistently share experiences with others online).

Example: L'Oréal originally targeted its Healthy Look Crème Gloss product toward a more mature female audience in search of a premium, non-permanent hair coloring solution. But sales data showed that the brand might have been missing out on a substantial opportunity among a younger audience more apt to experiment with color on a regular basis, and who are among a growing segment of "home dyers." So the brand launched "Play with Color," a collegiate marketing campaign that involved 70 female student influencers located on 35 campuses nationwide, who engaged students on their respective campuses.

This included hair coloring parties with sororities, fashion clubs, and dorm and apartment complexes; direct outreach through peer-to-peer communication and networks; and coupon distribution and social media contesting, which incentivized students to purchase the product and opt-in for brand communication going forward. There were guerrilla marketing tactics that allowed women to "play with color" without any true physical transformation via mirror clings in high-traffic women's bathrooms, all of which included calls to action that drove social media engagement.

Ultimately, these college Millennials were introduced to a new "accessory"—their hair—as something they could play with as part of a daily routine to change up their style and look good on any given day. They felt comfortable sharing the experience with peers and on social media and, given hair is kind of a big deal, with the proper education on the product most felt comfortable giving it a try. L'Oréal's program engaged 35,280 Healthy Look Crème Gloss coloring participants; 12,058 female students tried the Healthy Look product in groups through hair coloring parties, as well as the before/after hair color contests. L'Orèal distributed more than 300,000 Healthy Look Crème Gloss coupons, with a nearly 4 percent redemption rate.

- *Trial Connections.* Experiences that use the sample/trial of a product or service to engage and drive a connection with the target—usually a demo of a product or service is the bulk of the experience. These Trial Connections range from simple samples on a street corner or in a retail store, to the sophisticated trial of a new technology at a trade show, to a ride-and-drive program by an auto brand.

Example: After a decline in sales at Walmart, Gatorade decided it needed to reach bargain-hunting moms in a meaningful way. The company also wanted to push new messaging to its core teen consumers— male athletes who can and do make Gatorade purchases on their own, but also rely on their moms to pick up the product on their regular trips to Walmart.

Gatorade sent a fleet of Ford Transit vans, dubbed "G-Units," which were outfitted with slide-out sampling cages and built-in coolers, to more than 1,000 participating Walmart locations. Consumers walked up to the G-Unit and tasted the drink with a brand ambassador while viewing media content featuring professional athletes explaining the benefits of Gatorade's "Prime and Recover System"—a trio of drink solutions for active bodies. Afterward, they could take photos against a backdrop featuring an iconic Gatorade sports moment and have it printed as a custom Gatorade bottle label.

The key to the experience was the G-Tag Card game piece featuring a unique prize redemption code that could be scanned at special stations located at the Gatorade display inside Walmart stores. Upon scanning the card, a kiosk displayed what the consumer had won (from hats to sunglasses and other giveaways). The trick: The digital in-store display printed out a coupon that would be validated at the register with a purchase of Gatorade and then had to be taken back to the G-Unit in order to claim the listed prize, a strategy which generated sales spikes in addition to making Gatorade top of mind for the entire shopping experience. More than 1.5 million samples and consumer engagements were recorded, with sales spiking more than 500 percent on activation days, and often selling out the entire floor display in just one day.

- *Incentive Connections.* Provides an incentive to drive a target to participate and thus connect with the brand. For some companies, a simple discount is enough to drive a connection. Others provide a free giveaway or premium. The incentive can be small or large, and doesn't always have to have a monetary value. Many brands use exclusive event access and/or limited-edition content as incentives.

Example: Delta Air Lines gave consumers a taste of what its new $1.4 billion terminal at JFK airport had to offer with a pop-up called T4X in the SoHo neighborhood of Manhattan. The 6,000-square-foot retail space had two levels of real-life travel experiences, starting with Delta airport staff who helped consumers with "checking in" to Facebook from a custom iPad-based kiosk as they entered. The agents also assisted consumers who were actually flying with Delta that day to check in, upgrade their seats, or check their flight's status. Guests were e-mailed a "T4X boarding pass," which provided access to different stations, including a digital vending machine that dispensed Delta-branded giveaways. As an incentive for checking in, consumers were entered to win an all-expense-paid trip to one of Delta's international destinations.

Consumers could purchase lunch for $4 from an internationally inspired menu. The meals were delivered along a baggage carousel and packaged in a branded, luggage-like lunchbox. Visitors could eat or simply lounge on the second floor representing the new, elevated outdoor Sky Deck at Terminal 4, complete with projected digital aircraft flying overhead.

- *Movement Connections.* Using charities, causes, and collective community efforts to make a connection. Considered by many marketers to be the most organic and "pure" of the Experience Connection types. Movement Connections often create much more than a connection; they can create lasting ties in communities, and single programs have been known to drive connections between brands and targets that last longer than any other connection type.

Example: Less than 1 percent of girls express interest in majoring in computer science in college. Yet the tech sector is growing faster than any other industry. To champion this issue and be sure that the future of tech includes perspectives from women, Google created Made with Code, an initiative to inspire girls to try coding and be inspired to pursue a career in technology.

Google wanted a big stage to launch the initiative and engage girls in the campaign, so it partnered with the National Park Foundation and National Park Service to let girls bring the National Tree Lighting holiday ceremony to life through code. On a Made with Code website (madewithcode.com), girls could use an introductory coding experience to design the colors, patterns, and animation of the lights on one of 56 state and territory trees outside the White House.

Each girl's completed design was sent to Washington, D.C., incorporated in her selected state's tree-lighting scheme. She then received the date and the time when her design would light up. The 56 coded trees lit up alongside the National Holiday Tree at the annual televised event, each covered in 900 interactive LED lights that responded to the girls' designs, but also coordinated to light up in sync with one another. More than 2,000 people were in attendance, including many of the girls who coded trees, as well as the First Family, hosts Tom Hanks and Rita Wilson, and musical guests Ne-Yo, 5th Harmony, and Patti Labelle.

In addition to the event's ability to engage audiences with a Google cause, the brand made a $50 million commitment over three years to support an ecosystem of nonprofit partners exposing girls to computer science. In one month, with no paid media, more than one million digital trees were coded. The project received unanimous praise from mainstream press, including *The New York Times, Washington Post, Seventeen*, and *Mashable*.

CONTROL

One of the most debated subjects in experiential marketing is related to how much control a brand should exert over an experience and how much should be left to the audience.

Few elements have a greater impact on the success and failure of an experience than control does. If a brand asserts too much control, participants may not be as active and are often less inclined to participate. If a brand gives up too much experience control, it loses the ability to be the driver of the experience.

This "balance" has been debated for years by some of the biggest brands and smartest marketers. Research shows that participatory experiences drive longer and deeper connections. To create participation, there needs to be shared control. How much control to give and how much control to keep depend on the goal, the audience, and the comfort zone of the marketer. We've seen companies that use well-organized and detail-driven engagements with success, and others that relinquish complete control to their customers. Both are valid strategies and can yield impressive results.

There are five primary Engagement Control Structures (ECS) (Figure 3.1) that leading brands use to assert levels of control over experiences.

- *High Control Structure: Journey Sequencing.* Using deliberately designed paths to guide attendees through an experience. We've seen this also referred to as *continuum lines* and *experience mapping*. Journey Sequencing allows marketers to essentially put the target audience on a predefined and predesigned axis through a brand experience without participants feeling as if they're being guided or directed.

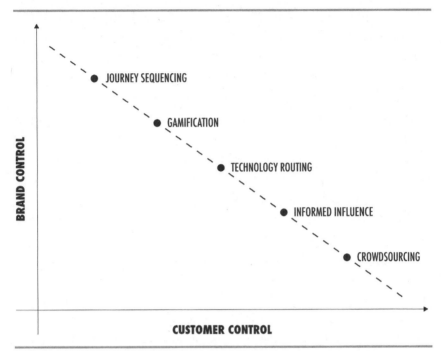

FIGURE 3.1   Engagement Control

Examples: Intel elevated the bar at the 2014 Consumer Electronics Show by creating a 14,500-square-foot "Digital Park" that demonstrated how its technology allows people to live an "untethered" life and showcased best-in-class smartphones, tablets, and Ultrabook devices with "Intel Inside."

An Ultrabook Tree attracted massive attention, both physically and through the media. The Tree featured 180 fully functional Ultrabook devices that served as a high-tech "digital canopy" above the space. Five Ultrabook Convertibles from Asus, Dell, Lenovo, Panasonic, and Toshiba surrounded the base of the tree. Guests created a digital "blossom" animation on one of the touch screens and launched them to the canopy with a drag-and-release function similar to that of "Angry Birds." Hundreds of LED lights on the front and rear of the tree trunk illuminated as the blossoms ascended and then bloomed into view and rippled across the canopy of Ultrabooks hanging like leaves on the techno-tree.

Just beyond the Ultrabook Tree canopy, a Digital Park offered guests the opportunity to watch presentations, experience the technology, interact with staff, or just relax and recharge. Framed by a multi-tiered terrace and with cirrus cloud formations overhead, the central focus of the park was the Spotlight Theater, where musicians, DJs, designers, and artists evangelized Intel technology, and interactive events involved the audience.

A second-floor hospitality lounge served as a spot for casual one-on-one meetings, blogging, and intimate group presentations. Non-traditional demonstration desks called "Petting Zoos" further emphasized the idea of "public space," along with interactive car- and bus-stop features, "street lights," and "grassy areas." Business took place away from the crowds in a two-story structure containing 13 meeting rooms.

Elsewhere, for the first time at E3, the largest annual trade show for the video game industry, Activision|Blizzard presented itself as a unified brand. The objective was to develop one brand experience and marquee billing of four game titles by transforming a space into an unprecedented, 4-D experience that attracted attendees and immersed them into the world of each game. With the help of agency NCompass International, the 17,000-square-foot space integrated first-class theatrical and technical production that took attendees on a jaw-dropping thrill ride. Dedicated spaces for each game offered a specialized experience, true to each game and its needs, while adhering to the Activision|Blizzard brand. Through a partnership with DIRECTV, consumers tuning in online could preview content shared with attendees through a "Call of Duty: Ghosts All Access" broadcast.

An immersive 190-degree, 122-foot by 22-foot curved screen—the largest stand-alone theater ever created in L.A. Convention Center history—drew attendees into the Activision|Blizzard world. Twenty-four projectors played uniquely choreographed shows for each of the four titles. The theater lit up into "attract" mode minutes before each show; "show" mode effects such as rumbling floors, wind, and smoke enhanced the experience for each game. Attendees interacted with the titles via hands-on gameplay or guided demos in four dedicated areas.

The 4-D experience, private screenings, social media interactives, and concierge-style reservations created a branded entertainment destination and a launch pad for sell-in through retail channels. Consumer preorders increased 232 percent.

- *Moderate-High Control Structure: Gamification.* Integrating elements of game playing (point scoring, competition with others, rules of play) into a brand experience. Allows marketers to talk less and play with an audience more. Studies show that when an audience enjoys an experience, memorability and inclination to buy rise. (Common sense tells us that when people are having fun, they want to stay, play, and engage longer.)

Example: Dodge used a month-long national campaign to increase awareness of its Journey crossover vehicle, which had not gained broad national market penetration when it debuted. To change that, the brand launched a digital offensive across Facebook, Twitter, a custom microsite, and YouTube, challenging consumers to get away from the computer and hit the road to find "the first search engine for the real world."

Dodge hid three vehicles, one in each of three geographic areas (west, central, and east), and then doled out clues on its YouTube channel, with each clue hidden in an understated ad-style video. The video clues pointed the way to real-world clues, hidden within each market. The contest progressed in three stages. Once the vehicle was found, the next contest could begin. The real secret was that the competitors couldn't just find the clues and know where the vehicle was hidden—they had to race to get there first and claim the prize in person. The idea, mostly promoted via viral buzz, caught on in a big way. In the first week alone, the YouTube channel had more than five million views, and each viewer spent an average of 25 minutes on the page. For the East Coast leg alone, there were thousands of consumers out on the roads, finding clues and searching for the prize, which was hidden near Port Clyde, Maine.

Gamification is also prevalent within business-to-business experiences. *Case in point:* If there's one thing all small business owners have in common, it's a competitive spirit. It's what drives them to turn their dreams into successful small businesses, and those successful small businesses into thriving competitors in their local markets.

American Express OPEN knows what makes these small business owners tick, so for its Consumer Electronics Show activation, the company created a gamification experience that brought that competitive spirit to life in an attention-getting—and lead generating—way.

The centerpiece of the experience was the Small Business Big Shot Game, an eye-catching 21-foot-tall branded tower that featured four custom-built LED-lit cubes. Each cube on the structure corresponded to a digital kiosk where trade show attendees competed in a trivia game on touch screens for a chance to win an iPad Air. The LED cubes visually demonstrated each participant's progress by moving up and down the tower with custom light animations, feeding their desire to outwit their competitors. The interactivity and visibility of the experience drove foot traffic to the OPEN booth and generated leads.

A seemingly simple concept (a multiplayer trivia game) was, in reality, quite a technological challenge. Not only did a multiplayer game have to be coded and set up in such a way that the four playing kiosks were in perfect sync, but the digital screens each had to control a physical object—the LED cubes—in perfect sync. In addition, lighting animations had to be programmed in the LED cubes, the cube height and style of movement determined, and it all had to be done in a way that kept the game even and fair to play. And all of this had to run continuously, for nine hours a day, during the four-day trade show.

Thanks to the huge physical presence of the Small Business Big Shot Game tower, American Express OPEN was able to generate the traffic it needed. Thanks to the gamification technology, folks stuck around. The combined effort resulted in over 1,800 game plays and generated over 1,600 leads for OPEN—as well as 100 percent of the new card acquisition goal.

- *Moderate-Low Control Structure: Technology Routing.* Using a series of technology platforms, interactives, and tech stations to capture an audience and then move that audience through a space. Often, the technology deployed allows a brand to manage how long and in what order that audience participates. Multiple technology engagements in a single experience provide marketers with the ability to control throughput (traffic), monitor engagement, and measure activity.

Example: To strengthen its sponsorship of collegiate sports, LG invaded the NCAA Final Four Fan Fest with a large, branded footprint. The 4,500-square-foot LG Training Facility was designed like a state-of-the-art university athletic training facility that gave fans the chance to be "recruited" by LG and learn how to "Do Game Day Right."

After registration, consumer "recruits" headed into the Player's Lounge, where they hung out on couches and interacted with LG products via a touch-screen game table, a tutoring center, and kitchenette, as well as a DJ area that featured LG's Music Flow speakers. LG integrated G Flex 2 mobile devices and LG curved OLED TVs into a gaming station in the space as well.

Fans continued into the Locker Room for a "pre-game experience" that featured glossy oak lockers stocked with uniforms and a custom-built digital interactive called the Speed Cycle Challenge, which put a twist on LG's laundry division's marketing messages "save time" and "larger loads." Consumers had 20 seconds to throw as many mini basketballs into an LG laundry washing machine as possible in a head-to-head competition. The appliances were configured with sensors hooked up to a digital scoreboard that counted the number of shots made.

Over in the private Practice Gym, more than 25 cameras (LG G3 mobile phones) captured participants doing their best dunk in 4K on an official NCAA Final Four basketball hoop. In the Film Room, they then reviewed their footage via a 105-inch Ultra HD 4K TV. Dunk highlights streamed from the gym courtesy of an LG/GoPro 4K rim cam.

At the conclusion of their "official visit," consumers were escorted out of the training facility through the Hall of Champions. The last engagement: a custom-built digital prize wheel where every fan spun using LG's gesture-control TV remote. What they landed on dictated the prizes they won, which included microfiber cloths, lanyards with ticket holders, compression sleeves, sweatbands, headbands, and $50 Lowe's gift cards.

- *Low Control Structure: Informed Influence.* Dating back to the theater experiences of the ancient Greeks in 700 B.C., the original low-tech control platform uses information to manage, guide, and assert control over where target audiences go, what they do, and for how long. As effective now as it was then, uses a well-communicated agenda and an experience design that uses information and content as the control platform.

Example: Microsoft's Worldwide Partner Conference (WPC) was reinvented with a new plan, a new experience, and a full strategic revamp based in easy, appropriate Informed Influence. A streamlined content story based on four major industry pillars drove the structure of the conference, from the keynotes, to the design of the expo floor, to the breakout sessions. More than 250 sessions were color coded based on the pillars—Big Data, Cloud, Devices & Mobility, and Enterprise Social—adding to a cohesive experience for the 14,000 paying attendees who came to hear what's next for Microsoft, how Microsoft was going to help them grow their businesses and, most importantly, to network. All content roads led to The Commons at WPC, an expo hall inspired by thriving city life and how modern business is conducted. A color-coded map on the backs of badges made navigating the territory easy, from the food service, moving inward through meeting areas, world regional lounges, neighborhoods of product solutions, to the event's City Center. There was also a series of "parklets" called the Low Line—which functioned like Manhattan's High Line—with turf grass and Adirondack-style chairs.

Microsoft found that, although turnover of companies attending WPC was not high, turnover of people was—about 30 percent of attendees each year are new. To ensure that first-timers had a productive experience, Microsoft began with digitalwpc.com, where a First Time Attendee page veteran partners offered tips and tricks, in addition to other resources. At the event there were meet-up spots and new-attendee luncheons, and designated seating areas at the keynotes, so newbies could network with other like-minded partners and Microsoft employees.

The cheapest and most effective aspect of the program? Red lanyards for new attendees and black for return attendees. Event alumni served as designated mentors, greeting first-timers and striking up conversations with them throughout the experience.

- *No Control Structure: Crowdsourcing.* The ultimate control surrender, when a brand turns over elements of the experience decision-making structure to the target audience. Typically allows an audience to create, suggest, or vote on aspects of a marketing campaign and is considered by many brands to be the most authentic of the five Experience Control Structures.

Example: While many marketers have preached the benefits of "turning the brand over to consumers," Mountain Dew and agency Motive turned its entire marketing mix over to them. For this campaign, consumers weren't just a target audience—they were the brand's chief marketing officers. The program kicked off in the month of July, and for 12 months it utilized Facebook, Twitter, YouTube, and live experiences to help guide and shape not only the next flavors of Mountain Dew, but the actual marketing mix. Consumers suggested, voted on, and selected the campaign's website look, product packaging, graphic design, advertising, event campaign strategy, and more. It was called DEWmocracy.

An initial online voting phase narrowed a field of flavors to three contenders. And the next phase became the foundation for one of the industry's greatest integrated online and offline experiential programs—the DEWmocracy Flavor Campaign that literally gave the reins of the campaign to millions of consumers who voted online and at hundreds of events across the country to elect one flavor into the permanent product lineup. The strategy leveraged the power of crowdsourcing to let consumers speak for themselves and, in the process, control an entire marketing campaign.

Hundreds of events were part "get out the vote" political rallies and part "Road Rules" challenges. Three teams of brand ambassadors, each representing—and evangelizing—one of the three flavors, set out across the country in branded mobile vehicles filled with samples and iPad voting stations, to stir up as much grassroots support and votes for their flavors as they could. Dew threw Flavor Rallies that spoke to the Dew community and represented the brand's unique personality in each market. There was very little pre-planning—each event was first sketched out in loose terms and then fans online helped the teams via "social routing" to determine what the right kind of event would be based on the flavor and the local audience. Each team was responsible for executing a series of 25 different activations. Dew laid out the challenge, and it was up to the teams to figure out how to activate the local communities to boost engagement and rock the vote.

The on-the-ground activations created a snowball effect, picking up momentum both online and off, as each group traveled across the country mixing grassroots marketing, street efforts, mobile tours, retail events, and more. In the end, each team logged more than 25 different interpretations of the same challenge in 69 cities, based entirely on what the fans wanted them to do. By the time voting wrapped up, more than 2.9 million votes had been cast and nearly 100,000 samples had been distributed amid hundreds of thousands of one-on-one engagements. The winning flavor was announced that June and hit store shelves in October. Sales spikes were immediate. The power of online and offline came together to drive brand, multiply reach, and boost ROI.

CONTENT

Some of the most effective experiential marketing strategies are designed to create content—in many cases, for the *rest* of the marketing mix. For most brands, the experience has become the greatest and most authentic generator and feeder of content. Trade show booths are serving as recording studios for YouTube videos. Keynote presentations at business-to-business events are being captured and redistributed as investor briefings, sales overviews, and employee messages. Entire Super Bowl TV spots are being filmed at events.

As one CMO told us: "Who needs an ad agency when you have experiential marketing?" Today's experiential campaigns are serving a variety of content roles. There are 25 types of content that leading brands are extracting from live experiences:

- *TV Spots.* Forget hiring actors and directors. Live experiences provide access to a real audience interacting in a brand experience.
- *Print, Direct, and Outdoor Ads.* Event environments are often so compelling that they can be featured in corporate print slicks, outdoor ads, banners, and so on.

- *Viral Videos*. The best viral videos capture random, unscripted moments—and those are the building blocks of events.
- *Social Media Posts*. There are no more content-rich sources for real-time or scheduled social media posts than events—they are the ultimate social media content feeders.
- *Employee Briefings*. Conferences and corporate meetings can be streamed or taped and used for internal employee communications.
- *Executive Roundtables*. At C-level events, putting CEOs in a room for on-the-record conversations can be repurposed into press materials, media articles, features, and blog posts.
- *B-roll*. With so much going on at events, there's no shortage of content to grab for your PR team's B-roll library.
- *Infographics*. Breakout sessions, keynotes, and Q&As provide fresh content for stat-driven or quote-based infographics.
- *Sales Training*. Packaging content from presentations into videos, webinars, web articles, and PDFs can form an action-packed product toolkit for sales.
- *Testimonials*. Chat with customers at the event—it can be the perfect place to capture them talking up your product or service.
- *Blog Posts*. There's a lot happening at events, and much of it can be written up as articles and columns for blogs. Don't forget to invite bloggers to the events so they can post to their channels.
- *Ebooks*. Content from events can be aggregated and laid out into an ebook for internal or external release.
- *Instruction Manuals*. The capture of launch events, product demos, or press demonstrations can be rolled up into instructional content for customers, sales reps, and other stakeholders.
- *Social Media Site Design*. From videos for YouTube channel headers to images for Twitter page backgrounds, event content is being used as imagery for social media page frames and skins.
- *Webcasts*. Event sessions can be streamed live or collected for future release as "digital classes" for internal or external audiences.
- *Photos*. Whether for Instagram, press materials, dealer catalogs, direct mail, or other marketing channels, events provide endless images . . . for endless uses.

- *Product Overviews*. From a CEO introducing a product, to a live demonstration of a product or service, "demo content" captured at events is showing up on morning talk shows, online, and across social media.
- *Live Media Interviews*. Events provide a broadcast experience like no other, which is why so many brands are building media studios into their event environments.
- *Vine Posts*. Six-second vids are all the rage, and there is a variety of "micro-content" available for capture at events.
- *Podcasts*. With a large number of attendees, speakers, and partners at events, it isn't difficult to recruit experts for live or taped podcasts.
- *Developer Communications*. Hackathons staged at events can be amplified in real time online or post-event with details released across developer blogs and message boards.
- *Slideshares*. The days of only distributing slides to attendees of b-to-b events are gone. Today's events push speaker slides to the cloud for amplified eyeballs and content reach.
- *Website FAQs*. Taking note of questions being asked by audiences at events provides a great perspective for website FAQ sections.
- *Investor/Analyst Briefings*. Event content can be packaged into or featured during financial calls, online videos, and shareholders communications. And don't forget: many investor and analyst meetings are now being produced within larger events.
- *Live Streams*. Only events offer a self-contained platform for amplified content. A single concert for 10,000 or keynote speech for 1,000—when streamed—can be seen by millions.

Example: Anheuser-Busch's Bud Light brand rewrote the book on content creation experiences with its Whatever USA program. The nation's top-selling beer brand had watched its core customer get older—and, in some cases, reach for the occasional wine or cocktail. In order to develop the Bud Light drinker of tomorrow, the brand needed to refocus on creating a new Bud Light drinker of today. So in a bold move, the beer giant reset its sights on a new audience: Millennials.

A new audience required a new message. So Bud Light created a new marketing platform, dubbed Up for Whatever. The campaign meshed perfectly with on-the-go, mobile Millennials, who are spontaneous, active, and always "up for whatever." This new Bud Light was, according to the tagline, "the perfect beer for whatever happens."

The initial Up for Whatever campaign was unveiled during the Super Bowl with a TV spot curated entirely from a documented evening out with a 27-year-old consumer who thought he was heading to a focus group, but instead found himself out for a wild night that included getting styled by Minka Kelly, defeating Arnold Schwarzenegger in sudden-death Ping-Pong, and going onstage with OneRepublic. The spot introduced a question that Bud Light would ask Millennials for months: Are you #UpForWhatever?

Within seconds of the Super Bowl spot airing, Twitter exploded. Millennials across the country hit the hashtag to let Bud Light know they were indeed up for whatever. Brand teams from handling agency Mosaic were standing by to turn those social hand-raisers into real-time content feeds—by first reverse-engineering their tweets to locate them and then serving up live experiences that could be captured and uploaded to Bud Light's YouTube channel.

A few examples: A consumer who tweeted he was #UpForWhatever as he ordered an Uber pick-up was met minutes later by a yellow Lamborghini. The driver even asked if he was up for whatever as the door opened. Another consumer who was watching the game at a bar while posting that she was #UpForWhatever had an entire halftime show, featuring singers, dancers, and EDM sensation Krewella, delivered to her—at the bar. The consumer who tweeted that he was #UpForWhatever from his own Super Bowl party had his party crashed minutes later by Hall of Famer Warren Sapp. It was all happening within minutes of the TV spot airing and being uploaded to social media in real time.

Welcome to the next chapter of experiential marketing, where the entire marketing mix—from above-the-line advertising to general marketing platforms to social media engagements—gets all content from live engagements. In the case of Bud Light's inaugural Up for Whatever unveiling, all content, from the TV spot to the surprise-and-delight social activations, was captured and posted online. And tens of millions of Millennials tuned in across YouTube, Twitter, and Instagram. While some brands spend months trying to figure out whether a campaign moved the needle, it took Bud Light mere hours to know it was onto something big.

The campaign extended into the winter/spring NBA season, with related Up for Whatever ads and viral content captured and posted. Millennials were responding across both the top and the bottom of the purchase funnel. With the critical summer selling season approaching, Bud Light saw an opportunity to take Up for Whatever to the next level.

In March, the decision was made to embrace a "win or go home" mantra. But to connect with Millennials (ages 21 to 27, split evenly between men and women) during the summer, when every brand was trying to connect with them, Bud Light had to create something that had never been created. The team needed to produce something most would label un-producible. Anything less than the Millennial experience of all Millennial experiences was unacceptable.

"Only if you push the boundaries will you know how far you can go," Bud Light VP Alex Lambrecht told us. "We had the courage to be bold."

What followed was the boldest summer initiative in the brand's history, a summer-long marketing program that would use tens of thousands of live events to connect with Millennials and engage those Millennials as the campaign's content source and amplifier. The premise: Bud Light would create an entire town—Whatever, USA—and Millennials who wanted to come for a weekend in September would have to prove they were #UpForWhatever all summer long.

The location of the town and exact details of the weekend were kept secret. Consumers went crazy for the idea. The buzz started in May. Media, PR, and digital/social efforts launched with a single message: "Bud Light is turning a real town into Whatever, USA, and you can come." A fictitious mayor of the town was featured across all marketing assets. The initial national campaign drove all engagements to UpForWhatever.com. Viral videos were released in stages, building word-of-mouth chatter for the overall campaign, Bud Light and, of course, the town. Since Millennials are hyper-digital, media buys were skewed 3:1 toward social and digital over TV placements. All content was designed and released with social sharing in mind, offering up constant opportunities for comments and viral redirects by Millennials.

By June, with the marketing machine officially flipped on, it was time to get face-to-face with consumers. Bud Light deployed more than 22,000 Whatever, USA–branded events to bars and nightclubs across the country. The heart of the on-site activation was an audition. Consumers who wanted a shot at attending Whatever, USA could pick up a (Bud Light blue) phone, which triggered a virtual interview with the mayor.

He'd ask one of 19 random questions. Examples included: "Based on your skills, what kind of world record do you think you could set?" or "What would your spirit animal be and why?" or "If you could do anything for a living, what would it be and why?" Consumers had 10 seconds to answer the question. The entire audition was captured and uploaded as a 15-second video to YouTube and that consumer's social networks—again, content being collected at live events and distributed everywhere else.

By August, it had become a phenomenon. Millennials chased the brand, begged for access to Whatever, USA, and shared more content than anyone had anticipated. More than 200,000 of them actually auditioned to get into Whatever, USA. In September, a final Last Call for Whatever event was held at 350 bars and nightclubs while the brand contacted, congratulated, validated, and booked 500 winners to go to Crested Butte, Colorado, which had been unveiled as the town that would be transformed into Whatever, USA.

For the entire summer, teams had been preparing the Colorado town for a transformation no brand had ever attempted before. Entire roads would be repaved; stores, restaurants, and hotels would be given makeovers; flight destinations would be altered. The logistics involved with getting the town to cooperate? Probably worthy of its own chapter. Some winners were notified via "selection day stunts" in which street teams hand-delivered larger-than-life Whatever, USA boarding passes to them while camera crews filmed and then uploaded the videos to YouTube. Each of the 500 winners could bring a friend, assuming they could get to their flights in less than 10 hours—they said they were up for whatever, *right*?

So three months and 22,000 events later, there was just one event left. Whatever, USA opened, serving as a bold finale to the summer program and a beacon to Millennials everywhere that the new Bud Light was the perfect beer... for whatever happens next. Because the winners were selected based on their personality, passion, social network, and influence power, they had large social networks and were predisposed to share—they just needed something worth sharing. Which is why Bud Light didn't create Whatever, USA for the 1,000 attendees—it created it for the rest of the world that would tune in to the content those 1,000 people posted. If provided the right experiences, those 1,000 attendees would feed Whatever, USA content to tens of millions of others. And they did.

From portal to portal, touchpoint to touchpoint, experience to experience, Whatever, USA came to life. Winners were flown to the nearby Gunnison, Colorado, airport in Whatever, USA–branded planes. They used Whatever, USA boarding passes to board the flights. Even the flight monitors at Denver International Airport were altered for their connections, listing Whatever, USA as an actual destination. When the buses from Gunnison crossed into Crested Butte, the consumers had arrived at Whatever, USA.

Bud Light transformed the entire town into a massive brand experience, with a level of detail rarely seen before. The town's famous Elk Avenue historic district was repaved Bud Light blue. All eight blocks of the town's merchants were given Bud Light makeovers—the Mountain Top Tees store became the Whatever General Store, the RM Chocolatier turned into Whatever Chocolates, and even the Avalon Salon became the Whatever Hair Salon, serving up free stylings. Elk Avenue restaurants were given menu tweaks and environmental touch-ups, from Bud Light artwork for the walls to design accents that added a little Bud Light to the establishment.

The main street merchant makeovers provided a branded backdrop to an overall schedule that was packed, stacked, and designed to be shared. There were more than 80 different events staged from Friday night through Sunday morning's farewell breakfast.

Much like consumers use a remote control to surf television shows at home, Whatever, USA guests used a branded app to stay on top of the busy schedule and choose what activities to engage in. At all times attendees could choose from multiple simultaneous events. Yoga at 10,000 feet, comedy improv, or kanga running? A bacon and Bud Light tasting, band camp, or sitting in a Jacuzzi while Questlove DJ'd? There were also what were dubbed "Stumble Upons," unscheduled encounters such as karaoke with Lil Jon and Vanilla Ice serving . . . vanilla ice cream.

"Millennials value experiences over material goods," says Lambrecht. "They want to be surprised, so the notion of not knowing what was around the corner was key."

The entire time, it was all being captured and shared by both Bud Light and the attendees. Video drones could be seen hovering at all hours while camera crews drove around town snapping photos for social media, shooting content for YouTube, and filming all of it for national TV spots. To help over-stimulate attendee tendencies to text, post, tweet, and hashtag, all guests were outfitted with RFID bands that triggered photos and videos that were shared immediately to their Facebook feeds and in a personalized Whatever, USA online photo gallery.

CURRENCY

Experiences have been called "the new currency of marketing," as customers and consumers have become more willing to initiate contact with brands in exchange for an experience. While many brand experiences charge admission and/or registration fees, some instead "charge" other types of behavioral or interactive Experiential Currencies.

We define Experiential Currency as when a target audience willingly provides something to, or engages in an interaction with, a company in exchange for an experience. As always, selecting and using the right Experiential Currency depends on the brand and the audience. Some customers are happy to engage in an experience in exchange for a chance to try a product. More elusive audiences are much harder to engage and may require exclusive content and access.

There are seven types of Experiential Currencies:

- *Trial Currency.* In order to gain access to or trigger a brand experience, a target is required to try a product or service. Try the product, get an experience.

Examples: Microsoft's Polished by Windows Phone campaign was as slick as the polish that was applied to participants' fingernails. The company's goal was to build awareness and consideration of Windows Phone 8 within Canada and connect back to its Meet Your Match campaign in the United States.

The holiday program focused on Canadian working moms. Setting up at shopping malls, Microsoft offered consumers a chance to escape from the hustle and bustle with an eight-minute mini manicure with the polish color of their choice while phone experts demonstrated the features of the Windows Phone 8. Tailored conversations compared the customer's current device to the Microsoft device, and participants received a free bottle of polish and a coupon for $50 off the new phone.

With their nails freshly polished, guests were invited to use the actual phone (trial) to enter the Next Windows Phone Hand Model contest. Microsoft reps took photos of their new manis and posted them to Facebook, where consumers could solicit votes through their social networks for a chance to win a two-day trip to Toronto, a hand model photo shoot with a $1,000 contract, and other prizes. Content was also shared on the social media sites of the shopping malls and Windows Phone Canada. Microsoft brought guys into the mix, too, with a Faceoff with Windows Phone contest that entailed posting messages and photos on multiple social platforms.

Consumers outside of Toronto and Vancouver could enter the Facebook contest by uploading photos of themselves holding a Windows Phone. For those who didn't own the phone, Microsoft posted a printable image of the phone on its Facebook page, so consumers could enter with the "proper" device.

The mall activation led to more than 2.5 million impressions and upwards of 7,500 manicures and Faceoff challenges. The contest reached six million consumers online during a five-week period, and more than 55 percent of consumers indicated they were more likely to recommend Windows Phone 8 after their experience.

Elsewhere, Scotch whisky marketer The Macallan created a small army of advocates who truly understand the brand. Macallan hosted free private tastings for consumers over four nights at The Altman Building in New York City. Each session of the Raise The Macallan campaign included 250 consumers who registered or had attended the brand's previous events. The select groups of hyper-engaged consumers were invited to be VIP guests with access to brand ambassadors, fine hors d'oeuvres, and a dram from a 12-year-old sherry cask. Consumers checked in at kiosks before the main show, unlocking a wireless connection and a custom-built site on their smartphone browser featuring a QR code they could use to participate in various experiences that night—a red-carpet-style photo shoot, a station where consumers were matched with Macallan labels and suggested food pairings based on their scent preferences, a trivia game, and more.

A brand ambassador presented a history of the whisky from a grand stage; during planned breaks in the presentation, servers handed out drams of The Macallan from different years. The ambassador described the aroma and flavor of each one, and then offered a toast.

- *Information Currency.* Requires an audience to turn over information about themselves or their company to gain access or admission to an event. We remember back at the 2005 Super Bowl in Jacksonville, Florida, Motorola made the bold decision to require a data-collect from all consumers who wanted to access its massive footprint at the NFL Experience fanfest. Consumers couldn't get in unless they completed a data-collection form the tech giant could use in its ongoing marketing efforts.

  Example: While consumers were waiting in line to get into Acer's two-store brand pavilion at the London Olympics, brand ambassadors approached them with Journey to Beyond Experience swipe cards that would unlock all of the interactives throughout the experience. But to receive the cards and get into the experiences, consumers had to complete a quick self-registration process on an Acer tablet—their personal data was their ticket into the experience. Guests inserted their cards into a reader at each station inside, and every time they did, they earned a point. When they accumulated 100 points, they could go online and register the card there to have a chance at winning a tablet of their own.

- *Behavioral Currency.* Exchanges admission or experience access for participation in a brand-specific activity.

Example: Smirnoff marketers set out to forge deeper relationships with its consumers through crowdsourced tasting experiences of its signature vodka. The vodka brand inspired 33,000 people around the world to submit party ideas on Facebook, picked the best ones, and then executed consumer-generated event concepts in 50 countries on the same night.

It was all part of the Smirnoff Nightlife Exchange Project, which gave consumers a forum for sharing ideas about their ideal nightlife events—the best of which Smirnoff would later bring to life. Consumers from 50 countries and six continents were invited to submit ideas via YouTube and Facebook and to vote on the best their countries had to offer. The best of the bunch were turned into live events all around the globe, all on one night. One added twist: Materials for each of the winning ideas were packed into crates and swapped between countries—so a great idea from Canada turned into a party in Brazil; a submission from Germany might create an event in Japan. Those who submitted the winning ideas won tickets to the events.

As a bonus, Smirnoff signed Madonna as the brand's dance ambassador. Dancers from across the world submitted audition videos on YouTube, and the best of the bunch were invited to audition for Madonna herself for a chance to dance on her next tour.

On the night of the events-around-the-world, the brand served about 117,000 Smirnoff cocktails, earned 5,000 Facebook "likes," and uploaded more than 8,000 photos to Facebook. Smirnoff's registered user and Facebook community grew by 375 percent, giving it the biggest online community of any spirits brand (8.5 million at the time). Nightlife Exchange earned media coverage in every market. The New York event alone generated PR hits in print and online, including in *People*, *Us Weekly*, and *Life & Style Weekly*. Press impressions for the campaign reached over one billion worldwide and sales spiked.

- *Intent Currency.* Also referred to as "hand-raiser currency," provides an experience to targets who say they are interested in buying a product or service. The automotive industry has been using Intent Currency for decades, trading intimate experiences for the all-important test drive.

Example: To introduce its high-end Cadenza, Kia partnered with OpenTable, the dining reservation website, and the high-end foodie website LuxeEpicure for a series of "dine and drives" that promoted its first entry into the premium car market. The eight-city Cadenza Experience tour began with a test drive of the Cadenza followed by a four-course meal prepared by a celebrity chef at a top-notch restaurant. At check-in, hand-raisers registered either to drive a Cadenza or be driven in one. After the drive, they gave their feedback on the experience and impressions of the car by filling out a survey. Those who opted in received a follow-up from a local Kia dealer. "The Cadenza launch signals a new era for Kia and provides an opportunity to engage and interact with consumers who may not have looked at the brand before in intimate and impactful environments," Michael Sprague, executive vice president of marketing at Kia, told us.

- *Social Currency.* Trades experiences for social media postings, shares, and mentions. There has been a substantial increase in experiences that require target audiences to "pay" for everything from product samples to meals and other services with a tweet or a social post.

Examples: British frozen food company Birds Eye opened a pop-up restaurant in London called The Picture House. There, diners could receive a meal from the brand's product line in exchange for posting a photo of their meal on Instagram with the hashtag #BirdsEyeInspirations.

Elsewhere, to build buzz for its summer merchandise, Old Navy turned to social currency and the hashtag #FlipFlopHurray, activating a Twitter vending machine stunt called Tweet for Your Feet that dispensed a free pair of flip-flops in exchange for a tweet. Vending machines were placed in Los Angeles and New York City at 36 high-traffic spots. (We've also seen Social Currency come alive across business-to-business events and meetings, with many offering discounts to registrants who tweet that they have signed up for an event.)

- *Admission Currency.* The traditional act of charging admission for an experience. Comes with the obvious benefit of revenue generation, and the indirect benefit of added targetability. After all, who would pay money to attend an experience they weren't interested in? (Put another way, charging for an experience allows a company to attract a fully relevant audience, as non-relevant targets wouldn't be willing to pay.)

Example: Bounty paper towels created Make-A-Messterpiece, a 10,000-square-foot pop-up experience in Chicago that was part brand experience, and part children's exploratory museum. Parents of children ages two and older paid $10 for an all-day stay, and special project stations and classes were an additional $5. The admission covered overhead costs such as utilities, materials, staffing, marketing, and stocking a retail boutique and café. "We are covering some of the operating costs with the investment we put in, but the revenue generated helps offset that, which definitely gives us more of a right to succeed in this area," Chris Brown, Bounty brand manager, told us.

• *Transaction Currency.* Rewards customers who make a purchase with an experience (or a series of them). Typically, brands heavily promote the experience in an effort to motivate the target audience to make a purchase. Transaction Currencies provide buyers with exclusive experiences that inspire loyalty.

Examples: Camp RZR was a three-day off-roading Mecca for Polaris RZR owners and their families that took place in the desert of Glamis, California. There, buyers of the product could experience miles of open sand and Polaris hospitality at its best—along with a big, roaring thank you from the brand. The extravaganza—which kicked off with a Halloween night trick-or-treat—offered free food, contests and giveaways, celebrity fun-ride competitions, stunt expos, demo rides, movie nights, a kids' play area, fireworks, customization competitions, and free mechanical support for all Polaris owners.

A full lineup of activities kept the crowd hopping. A second mobile RZR Experience Tour made an official stop at Camp RZR, with two crews running at all times to get as many attendees as possible into the new RZR XP 1000 side-by-side vehicle. It had to be the best demo ride ever offered in the dunes. A Show & Shine contest awarded prizes for the Best of Show, Best Paint/Graphics, Best Electronics, and Craziest Build. The grand finale of Camp RZR was a RZR XP 1000 giveaway.

The RZR Experience attracted 30,000 participants and the most demos of any of their eight stops, plus strong media coverage.

Elsewhere, music fans want VIP access, and Citi wanted its customers to know it cares, so the company used its sponsorship of The Rolling Stones 50 & Counting Tour to promote Citi Private Pass, which rewards card members with exclusive perks. The brand entertained top Citi customers and VIPs as well as friends and family of the band in a custom VIP Lounge at each tour venue. Some guests even got a shot at a backstage tour or a meet-and-greet with The Rolling Stones. Activations started just a few days before the tour, and the pre-announcement action focused on the hashtag #StartMeUpWednesday, which pulled in more than 27.3 million impressions and reached more than 5.3 million individual users on Twitter . . . in a week. The VIP Lounge at each show hosted Citi guests and friends of the band and offered food and an open bar decked out in Glam Rock style right up until the Stones started playing. A custom retro photo booth was incorporated into the Citi VIP Lounge, and guests took photos and printed them out as keepsakes of the once-in-a lifetime experience. Ten or so fans had the chance to meet The Stones themselves, surely a lifetime memory.

What's more, in just eight weeks the brand scooped up more than 747 million social impressions and the official Stones app, presented by Citi, had more than 15 million page views.

CONVERSION

We always remind marketers who attend our training events that the only thing that matters in marketing is conversion. Creating conversion is the ultimate objective of a brand experience.

The insights and examples we share in this book are culled from thousands of marketing strategies and conversations with some of the most effective users of experiential marketing. But if you can finish this book with one takeaway, let it be this one: That all experiential marketing roads lead back to conversion and that the ultimate goal of a brand experience is to convert "someone" into "something." A buyer. An advocate. An employee. A follower. A friend. A lifetime customer. There are seven Experience Conversion Platforms:

- **Sales Conversion.** The use of live experiences to convert somebody into a buyer and generate sales of a product or service. This is the most common Experience Conversion Platform.

  Example: L'Oréal Paris is so committed to engaging women in new and innovative ways that nothing can stand in its way—not even the New York City subway system, where it installed an "intelligent" vending experience beneath Bryant Park that stopped women in their tracks and placed L'Oréal at the forefront of emerging virtual shopping trends. The L'Oréal Paris Intelligent Color Experience became the first-ever intelligent shopping experience in the New York City subway system.

  When a woman approached the activation, she immediately saw her reflection in a custom-built full-length mirror overlaying a digital display. A proprietary color detection algorithm using cameras and proximity sensors analyzed her reflection and detected the colors of her outfit. As she looked at her reflection, she saw particles of detected colors coalesce into a recommended palette of three of her most prominent colors. This palette transitioned to the shopping experience, where she received recommendations for hand-selected cosmetic packages to match or clash with her outfit and could buy them on the spot, right on the subway platform.

- **Pipeline Conversion.** Effectively using experiential marketing for the purposes of demand-generation (lead-generation).

  Examples: The U.S. Army had to get high-tech to fill its quota of 80,000 new recruits. To that end, it created the Army Experience Center, housed in the Philadelphia Franklin Hills Mall. The experience incorporated an incredible amount of technological gadgetry, but the highlight was an interactive augmented reality game that put players and prospective soldiers into the gunner's seat of a Humvee or attack chopper. To enter, guests registered and were set up with a photo ID that incorporated an RFID location-tracking card. They were then instructed to swipe the card at each interactive inside. In the video gaming area, attendees played an Army-designed game that tracked not only time spent playing, but also what job the players chose and how well they did, in real time. The appropriate recruiter could then engage them and chat about their specific interests and performance within the game.

Elsewhere, at Salesforce's gigantic business-to-business Dreamforce event, CRM tools measure the dollar opportunities represented by the customers who are planning to attend. "We know down to the penny what exactly in terms of pipeline the show represents to the company, and we have a target for the pipeline going into the show and a target for the pipeline that will be generated from those attendees in the 90 days following, and a target for the close rate on that," senior VP-strategic events Elizabeth Pinkham told us.

- *Influencer Conversion.* Brand experiences designed to connect with a smaller group of targets who will then share that experience with others and effectively "infect" their friends and family with the experience or intended message of it.

Example: Unilever's Axe personal care brand found an ideal way to link its shower gel with consumers' interest in conservation and the environment. The brand, which targets young men ages 18 to 24, came up with the idea of Showerpooling—sharing a shower with multiple people. The campaign was based in part on research findings that Millennials are 69 percent more likely to consider a brand's social and environmental commitment when deciding what products to buy, and they are 83 percent more likely to trust a brand if it is socially and environmentally responsible.

Axe put that knowledge to use by focusing on their commitment to water conservation while engaging college students with practical tips and resources they could use to make an impact on the issue in their local communities. The Showerpooling experience hit college campuses via a 10-market tour that included sampling, distribution of water-efficient showerheads, and a celebrity media launch event at the University of Southern California. TV and web ads rounded out the campaign.

While the initiative promoted Axe Shower Gel, the real hero of the campaign needed to be water conservation, which led to messaging drawn from Unilever's sustainability division and the Alliance for Water Efficiency. Games and activities encouraged students to take Axe's pledge to use less water. Axe collected e-mail addresses during the campus activation and e-mailed students a link to take the Showerpooling Pledge on Axe's Facebook page. The online campaign included content from the college tour and an opportunity for Axe fans to engage with the program.

In all, more than 10,000 students participated in the on-campus activation, and the brand collected more than 8,000 student e-mail addresses and delivered 300,000 product samples. Purchase intent during the campaign increased 14 percent.

- *Mention Conversion.* Using experiences to communicate with and impact the press/media. Social media efforts used to generate posts and shares across social platforms also fall under the Mention Conversion platform.

Example: Journalists who write about cars have probably "been there and done that" when it comes to ride-and-drives and press events. But they likely experienced a first at the Nissan 360 event, which promoted the business direction of the company and its Nissan, Infiniti, and Datsun brands. Attendees were offered the chance to drive more than 100 vehicles. Nissan invited 1,000 journalists from around the globe for the three-day experience in Newport, California, designed to demonstrate strategies, showcase technology, and impress auto journalists.

On each of two mornings, journalists were shuttled to the El Toro Proving Grounds with eight unique tracks and 130 vehicles on hand to drive or ride in. Three tech centers displayed innovations and an air-conditioned 13,200-square-foot tent acted as the main Pavilion, where there were displays for the Nissan, Datsun, and Infiniti brands and six concept vehicles. The Pavilion also featured a 100-seat theater that hosted more than 42 top company executives across all three brands, as well as press conferences. Then came the nights—a champagne toast of Nissan's 80 years over a sunset; a gala highlighting design with five-star dining; and an All-American beach party with hamburgers and cold beer served out of the back of Nissan pick-ups.

Technology and a mobile app helped guests keep track of the schedule and events. They could receive information on products and vehicles by tapping RFID-enabled displays. They could also schedule off-site street drives with vehicles and get turn-by-turn GPS directions back to the raceway. As a result, there was very little signage other than minimal directionals, and no brochures were handed out at the event. Any information the guests wanted was downloadable to their personal "virtual briefcases." Nissan felt it had a critical story to tell, and attendees listened. Most attendees took on average 10 test drives, with a total of 15,000 test drives recorded. The event earned nearly 31 million social media impressions, including more than 1.2 million impressions from bloggers and online media coverage.

- **Retention Conversion.** When companies use experiences for the purpose of maintaining an ongoing dialog and relationship with current customers—the overarching goal is to stimulate future repeat purchases.

Example: With its Catalyst Mobile Education Center, Medtronic created a fully functional mobile campus that enables the company to bring surgeons the latest techniques and most advanced technology.

The mobile centers travel throughout the United States to hospitals, orthopedic clinics, and teaching universities to instruct surgeons and doctors in the proper use of Medtronic spinal tools and devices. The multi-functional trailers are outfitted with cutting-edge procedural/ anatomical labs, conference areas, a restroom, and four changing areas where doctors can prepare for lab work.

One trailer houses the conference areas and a state-of-the-art audiovisual system that features large-screen monitors used for meetings and demonstrations. The second trailer contains six workstations with laboratory space to accommodate up to 60 surgeons at a time and is equipped with instrumentation, fluoroscopes, surgical and navigation systems, and more.

The initiative has become an essential program for introducing new products, technology, and treatments to surgeons nationwide in a real-life setting.

- *Awareness Conversion.* The use of brand experiences to drive pure awareness for a product, service, brand, or marketing message. Typically, focus is on reaching the most people, not on sales.

Example: It's not always easy getting everyone in the room—family, especially—to agree on what to watch on television, but during a holiday season Netflix set out to prove it could serve as the common denominator. While millions of consumers are subscribing to streaming services that allow them to curate television viewing rather than be subjected to unwanted channels and commercials, many still don't understand how it works.

The Netflix Family Room in-mall campaign targeted primarily non-Netflix users passing through popular shopping areas in Los Angeles, New York City, Chicago, and San Francisco for two weeks during the holiday season.

The 12-by-15-foot spaces looked like a typical American living room with a fireplace and comfortable chairs. Consumers entering the space could grab a seat and watch streaming holiday movies, take holiday photos with props, or wrap some of their purchased gifts at a gift-wrapping station. Brand ambassadors outfitted in holiday sweatshirts engaged consumers with iPads to share how to use, sign-up, and give Netflix as a gift, as well as answer questions from existing customers.

All of the experiences were "no obligation," meaning guests didn't have to register to participate. Netflix wanted to provide positive interactions with the brand, rather than conduct surveys and collect data. It did measure interactions, including 23,773 living room engagements and 26,120 product demonstrations. (There were 12,811 gifts wrapped, too.)

- *Human Capital Conversion.* One of the most effective but least discussed Conversion Platforms. Uses brand experiences to engage, inform, and communicate with employees or stakeholders.

Examples: DIRECTV's mobile Learning Experience Lab visited its customer-care call centers across 31 states to help make agents comfortable discussing the advantages of its products over increasingly popular streaming services. The ultimate goal was to lay the groundwork for more customers to upgrade to DIRECTV's premium and sports packages. But to do that, customer service reps needed to be familiar with the company's changing competitors—streaming services and the devices customers use to access them.

Each lab environment remained on-site for one week. The lab incorporated seven teaching stations that used instructional videos, learn-by-play activities, and one-on-one instruction designed to show agents product comparisons so they could understand the shortcomings that customers would experience with competitive products. A center island displayed DIRECTV applications on tablet devices and smartphones, and in the back, larger groups of agents could receive instructor-led product and program demonstrations on a 60-inch TV. The brand attributed $8 million in incremental revenue to the program.

Elsewhere, at its Global Leadership Conference, Starbucks focused on strengthening connections with the 10,000-plus store managers and regional managers who serve customers daily. For the four-day conference in Houston, the brand's goals were to create unforgettable experiences that reinforced the company's message of leadership across the business and to inspire the team to take the next step on the Starbucks journey.

Two general sessions at the Toyota Center bookended the four days. A theater-in-the-round concept engaged the audience with guest speakers, two coffee tastings (9,500-plus cups distributed in under six minutes), keynote speeches by historian Nancy Koehn and the Rev. Calvin O. Butts, multiple appearances by Starbucks Chairman and CEO Howard Schultz, and a performance by Grammy Award winner Alicia Keys. The 400,000-square-foot experiential Leaders' Lab in the adjacent George R. Brown Convention Center explored the complex situations and interactions that make up a manager's daily life. Using analog and digital media and hands-on and interactive experiences, the Lab celebrated the brand and engaged attendees.

To reinforce the message that Starbucks cares about its communities, attendees participated in daily activities helping to rebuild Houston's Fifth Ward. The company also provided bus service to Houston restaurants each evening, creating a meaningful impact on local businesses.

On the event's last day, Houston's Discovery Green Park was the setting for a whirlwind of experiences that included food trucks, an art walk and craft fair, and multiple stages with entertainment from multiple genres. The party not only capped the conference but also allowed participants to relax, connect, and talk about their conference experiences.

STRATEGY FIRST

The best brand experiences are grounded in a strategy, and the best strategies are developed before the idea, the design, and the look and feel. By combining objectives and insights first, marketers can begin to develop experiential marketing endeavors that benefit both the business and the brand.

Chapter Four Anatomy of an Experiential Marketing Campaign

Highly evolved experiential marketers tend to deliver amazing results rather consistently. We've analyzed thousands of experiential campaigns over the past decade spanning virtually every product and service category imaginable, and we've concluded that success is not dictated by company size, longevity, manpower, or even budget. Rather, the truly great campaigns share the same anatomy, which is composed of 11 Experiential Pillars. These pillars are the essential building blocks of successful experiential programs. As with a great recipe in which ingredients are blended together to create a unique flavor, these pillars work together to optimize engagement and will allow you to achieve the brand-building, value-creating, clutter-breaking power of experiential marketing. When we analyzed more than 1,000 winners of our global Ex Awards recognition program, we found that successful campaigns are built on 11 Experiential Pillars, shown in Figure 4.1.

REMARKABLE

In Chapter 6 we'll discuss the essential rules of theatrical engagements that apply to experiences. Rule 3 is that a grand entrance has impact. This rule is central to making your experience remarkable. An experiential

FIGURE 4.1 The 11 Experiential Pillars

program is a live opt-in event, so your presence must be designed to cause your target audience to choose to deviate from their path and give their time to you. Time is your biggest obstacle, and the easiest way to overcome it is to make your presence so spectacular that your targets can't help but take notice and participate.

"If it's not remarkable, it will be invisible," Dan Griffis, Target's VP of Experiential Marketing, told us. Over the last few years, no retailer has embraced experiential marketing like Target has. The company has wired live experiences throughout its marketing mix. From sponsorships and grassroots marketing to guerrilla efforts and beyond, Target's programs are simultaneously national and local, in-store and out—and amplified online and offline.

There's a science to it all. Engage the consumer the right way and you make a connection. If it's the right connection, you can generate a conversion—effectively turning that consumer into a Target shopper. In recent years, Target has added more focus—and more experiential marketing dollars—on the fickle, elusive, distracted, and all-important college student.

Since lifetime shopping preferences are imprinted early, it's becoming more critical to connect with consumers earlier, and more frequently. As a shopper segment, college students are style-focused and budget-minded, perfect for Target's overall wheelhouse. They're also connected to digital and mobile devices—the perfect target.com shoppers. And for a seasonal revenue opportunity, college kids make up a hefty chunk of back-to-school-related purchases.

So with the goal of amping up efforts to connect with the college collective, Target and its agency Deutsch created a back-to-school program that would make connections, increase affinity, and drive sales. The challenge was that Millennials thought of Target as the place their moms shopped. Which meant that, in order to change that perception, Target would have to change their behavior.

And indeed they did, with Bullseye University Live, a 360-degree experiential campaign that connected with both masses and individuals online and on the ground. It was part reality show, part digital experiment, and total marketing genius, a textbook case in integrated marketing that incorporated social media, pop-ups, content, and a drive to retail that left no stone unturned in the quest to get college students tuned in to Target during the $80+ billion back-to-school shopping season.

"While we know students are increasingly relying on digital experiences, we also know that they crave interaction and remember more from a physical experience than they do from just reading or hearing something," Griffis told us.

It began with a national experiential effort that eventually went hyperlocal. Target built a multi-story Bullseye University dormitory experience and set it up on the UCLA campus over the summer. Once each room was "curated" with Target décor and merchandise, five of YouTube's most popular video personalities moved in. Together, the "roommates" had five million followers. Target live-streamed their antics 24 hours a day on bullseyeuniversity.com as they whiled away the four days in those dorm rooms filled floor-to-ceiling with Target merchandise. The digital denizens interacted with followers across social media and hyped the goods inside their rooms. The best part: By scrolling over the products, online viewers activated pop-up boxes with additional information and links that allowed them to make instant purchases.

The anchor of the structure was a ground-level lounge that was taken over by a different brand—Ben & Jerry's, Zip Car, Champion, Beats by Dr. Dre—each day. Each hour of each day was programmed with "socially fueled" content (such as a workout class or a magic show) that kept student viewers coming back to watch . . . and shop. Over the four days, college students across the country tuned in for an average of nearly 12 minutes. The activation generated 76 million Twitter impressions.

A month later, the national experience went hyperlocal. To sustain the message that Target was the one-stop shop for back-to-college essentials, two-day Bullseye University Live pop-ups were set up during "move-in week" at five campuses to create a real-world extension of the interactive digital experience college students were first introduced to via the streaming event. To best showcase the back-to-college products and practical dorm room solutions Target provided, a dorm room "resident" dined, lived, and played in the structure for 48 hours while thousands of students on each campus came by. A key focal point of the dorm room was a 70-inch, motion-sensor touch screen that allowed students to play games and interact with the dorm room.

At each campus, the two-day program featured activities and content tied to Target's house brands along with those of 10 brand partners, including SC Johnson, Wrigley, Maybelline, Sally Hansen, Coca-Cola, BIC, and Pepperidge Farm.

Programmed as if it were a live television channel, each hour had a different brand activating in a new way. "The goal was to create an experience that was cool enough to get students to lift their heads from their phones," says Daniel Chu, the Deutsch experiential team's executive VP and creative director.

The dorm room itself was filled with the season's best trends in room décor and all the essentials college kids needed. Students could check out the items in the dorm room and then visit a QR code shopping wall on the side of the live dorm room to scan and purchase items directly from their phones.

If students needed to grab their last-minute items immediately, Target provided shuttle buses to run students back and forth to the nearest store. On some campuses, students could even purchase products onsite. At each touch point, they were reminded that all of the essentials they need could all be found in one place: Target.

Target integrated each school's colors and traditions to make the Dorm Room a part of campus life. From the "Howdy" at Texas A&M to the Tiger Walk at Auburn, the retailer integrated school spirit into the experience. Each day, the dorm room's décor was changed to feature a boys' and a girls' room to allow students to see the variety of merchandise available at Target.

In less than a month, the Bullseye University Live Dorm Room reached 144,000 students and parents at the five colleges, pushing engagement to the next level, generating real-time sales, and changing both perception and behavior.

SHAREABLE

The essence of an experience is that it is something special that compels people to share with others. This presumes that you have something to say and that your message is worth sharing. Not only are the best experiences shareable, but they also are shared. In other words, the experience is enhanced when it is experienced in group settings. This is why, even in the age of Netflix, when we can watch a movie in the comfort of our own homes, we still enjoy going to theaters and experiencing the same film in a group setting.

Most marketers understand the importance of creating memorable moments and content worth capturing and sharing across digital channels. Over the next few years, more consumer and business-to-business marketers will focus their efforts on developing engaging event content strategies to earn increased social engagement from targeted fans.

Research from the Event Marketing Institute indicates that marketers' primary social engagement goals are to drive attendance and then reach attendees on-site during events. A secondary, emerging trend, which many leading companies are already focusing on, is to reach stakeholders, prospects, and influencers who may not attend the events.

The importance of marketing social content is also suggested in the finding in a study commissioned by experiential agency FreemanXP with the Event Marketing Institute that 50 percent of leading event marketers have a specific budget for viral efforts (February 2015). In addition, 53 percent of brands are increasing their spending on social efforts.

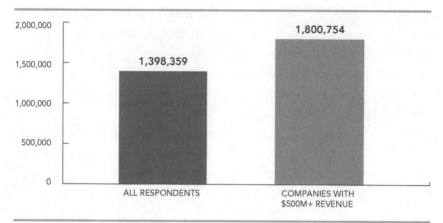

FIGURE 4.2   Total Viral Reach, Per Event
Source: The Viral Impact of Events, EMI/Freeman XP

Viral Reach

Figure 4.2 provides the estimated total touches, communications, connections, and impressions about the brand, event, or exhibit activity. Clearly, the viral impact, especially seen by large companies, is significant. The survey question was: *Considering your largest, most important event or exhibit, please estimate the total viral impact and word of mouth generated by your online and social media efforts. That is, please estimate the total number of viral touches, communications, or connections about your brand, exhibit or event presence.*

"Viral Impact Estimate" Confidence Level

The survey asked respondents to rate the level of confidence they had in their estimate. A total of 46 percent had an 80 to 100 percent confidence level for their estimates. Still, 14 percent said their confidence level was under 50 percent, and 25 percent indicated they had no idea and were simply guessing at the impact.

An analysis of the companies that indicated they had 100 percent confidence in their viral impact found a very significant average figure of *7.8 million* touches, communications, connections, and/or impressions. Nearly all of the companies reporting 100 percent confidence have over \$500 million in revenue. Most of these companies are in technology sectors with their own events and social engagement strategies specifically targeted to non-attendees, often around the world. These leading companies are truly focused on extending and amplifying their live experiences.

Effectiveness at Generating Viral Impact and Content Sharing from Event Programs

The survey findings suggest that marketers feel they could be more effective with their viral efforts. Consider that only 16 percent say they are "very effective" at generating viral impact. Analyzing the data further finds that companies serving both business and consumer markets, which are often large companies in IT, medical, and financial sectors, feel they are the most effective at generating viral impact.

Extending and Amplifying Event Marketing Programs via Social Media

Extending and amplifying event programs via social media was "extremely" or "very important" to a total of 70 percent of top companies and brands. Event-related social marketing is most important to companies with over \$500 million in revenue. Figure 4.3 shows this comparison.

HOW IMPORTANT IS SOCIAL AMPLIFICATION	ALL RESPONDENTS	OVER \$500M
Extremely important, critical	32%	47%
Very important	38%	30%
Somewhat important	21%	17%
Not very important	8%	7%
Not at all important	1%	0%
Other	0%	0%

FIGURE 4.3 Importance of Social Amplification
Source: The Viral Impact of Events, EMI/Freeman XP

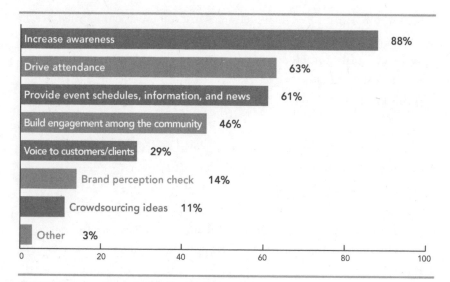

FIGURE 4.4   Social Media: Pre-Experience
Source: The Viral Impact of Events, EMI/Freeman XP

Importance of Social Amplification

Pre-Event Social Media

As you see in Figure 4.4, social media is mainly used before events and experiences to increase awareness, drive attendance, and provide general information. Analyzing survey data by market segment finds that 65 percent of companies that serve both business-to-business and consumer markets also focus their pre-event social efforts on building engagement among their market community.

How Social Media Is Used During Events

During events, social media is mainly used to promote event elements or features as well as to share photos and content. About one-third of companies do one or more of the following while onsite at events and exhibitions: promote education and content, promote contests/giveaways, amplify product announcements, and measure the experience and access feedback (Figure 4.5).

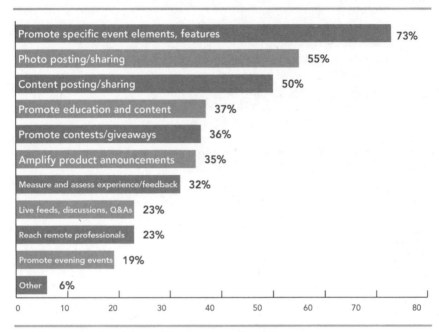

FIGURE 4.5   Social Media: During Experience
Source: The Viral Impact of Events, EMI/Freeman XP

Post-Event Social Media

Following events, about half of event marketers use social channels to relive or summarize highlights and leverage influencers. In fact, the largest companies (those with over $500 million in revenue) place a much greater emphasis on leveraging influencers, often those with large or important followings, with their post-event communications. Figure 4.6 provides this comparison. In fact, leveraging influencers is the most common post-event social engagement activity among larger companies.

Coke Shares Happiness

Happiness is always better shared, and through its "Share a Coke" campaign, Coca-Cola took this idea to the next level. Many consumers rely on connection technologies such as e-mail and social media as a substitute for human connection, and Coca-Cola sought to resolve this through a shared, personal experience. Coca-Cola hit the road with the

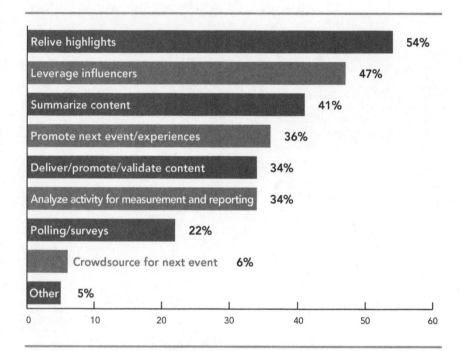

FIGURE 4.6   Social Experience: Post-Event
Source: The Viral Impact of Events, EMI/Freeman XP

mission of allowing everyone in America to create his or her own personalized can of Coke, as well as another for a friend.

The Share a Coke campaign surpassed even Coca-Cola's vision, delivering more than one million personalized Share-a-Coke cans over the course of 500-plus stops across the United States, with an additional 700,000 social media posts generated as a result of the campaign's content.

"Experiential marketing gave us the opportunity to reach millions of our most loyal drinkers who wanted to participate in the Share a Coke movement but couldn't find their names in stores. It helped us to deepen that relationship in a truly meaningful way, and the 'shareability' of the events allowed that reach to extend beyond the actual events and connect with millions more through authentic social media interactions," Coca-Cola Marketing Director Evan Holod told us. The brand enjoyed a 2 percent lift during the promotional window.

MEMORABLE

To be memorable, an experience must have elements of surprise and delight, but also provide a context to support the message or "content" that you want your participants to remember and share. Experiences are memorable when the participants can say, "I learned something," "I discovered something," "I created something," "I saw something," or "I met someone." Experiential marketing pros create the "somethings" and "someones" to ensure their programs resonate even after the experience ends.

WestJet's Holiday Surprise

Canada's WestJet Airlines created a memorable experience for holiday travelers that turned a surprise and delight experience into a social media sensation that exceeded all PR, awareness, and brand-perception goals.

Holiday travel is often hectic, and airports tend to be the last place we expect to feel happy—unless we're leaving them. To create a memorable and lasting experience for 250 passengers, WestJet and agency Mosaic activated the holiday "Christmas Miracle." The carrier set up kiosks at two international airports for two Calgary-bound flights. Passengers scanned their boarding passes, prompting a live video stream of a virtual WestJet Santa Claus asking them—by name—what they wanted for Christmas.

In WestJet's nearby Digital Command Center, a team of more than 150 volunteer "WestJetters" became Santa's Helpers, and purchased and wrapped personalized gifts for all the guests while they were airborne en route to Calgary. When the passengers got off the plane and headed to baggage claim, they discovered a holiday paradise with decorations and lights. Then, they watched as the festively decorated carousel roared to life and brought down not just their luggage, but also the gifts that each had requested merely hours before. One passenger even received a flat screen TV.

Nineteen hidden cameras captured the experience and guests' reactions from departure to arrival. The video was unveiled on WestJet's YouTube page, which set off a viral sensation. The brand offered to provide free flights to reunite families in need through its longtime partner,

Ronald McDonald House Charities, once the video reached 200,000 views. The brand followed up with a carefully crafted communication plan involving social media, press releases, and a broadcast media tour to spread the video's love.

The video received 35 million views on YouTube and was one of the most watched viral ads of the year worldwide, exceeding the brand's goal of 500,000 views by 7,000 percent. In addition, WestJet reported revenue increases of 86 percent, boosts in bookings of 77 percent, and visits to WestJet.com up by 100 percent.

Heineken's Standout Sponsorship

Heineken is a leader in using highly visible sports sponsorships as a platform for connecting with enthusiasts in a way that enhances their fan experience. Heineken was looking to leverage its Union of European Football Associations (UEFA) sponsorship in a remarkable way and become part of the online conversation in social media around the Champions League Final. Working with agency partner TBWA Amsterdam, Heineken discovered that the UEFA championship game fell on the same day as the opening of Ibiza's party season. So Heineken devised an experiential program that brought the excitement of Champions League Football and Ibiza-style partying together for the first time in a consumer experience that combined spectacular beach activities and entertainment, watching the Final on a big screen against an ocean backdrop, and Ibiza's famous parties. With all of that, plus football celebrities in attendance and live streaming on social media channels, it was sure to connect with its target audience—its so-called "Man of the World" consumers, ages 25 to 34, from around the globe, who love music, sports, and new adventures. Heineken's Ibiza Final experience delivered on the brand's desire to become part of the online conversation in social media around the Champions League Final.

With famous footballers reporting live from the Ibiza spectacle and providing live match commentary, Heineken significantly outperformed other Champions League sponsors. It achieved a 75 percent share of voice on Twitter and drove 130 million social media impressions around the final match. "These days, it's all about finding unique insights to develop unique experiences, and then showcasing these to a global audience. And that is exactly what we did," Roeslan Danoekoesoemo, global sponsorship manager at Heineken, told us.

MEASURABLE

Experiential marketers know the value their programs create because they build measurement criteria into their campaigns from the start. Chapter 7 provides a deeper dive into measurement strategies and methodologies, but the programs that follow show how marketers in vastly different categories are able to prove performance.

SAP Uses Insights to Go Small

Like many large enterprise software companies, SAP hosts numerous events around the world to bring together its customers, partners, employees, and other stakeholders to share ideas, stimulate business, and create and enhance relationships. SAP was looking to take key learnings from the overhaul of its flagship global event, SAPPHIRE NOW, and create smaller, more personalized customer experiences.

Reminiscent of popular "total takeover" consumer events, SAP executed a complete buyout of conference venues and facilities, including restaurants, bars, coffee shops, and gift shops, and transformed them into brand experiences for its newest event property: SAP Select. This unique approach allowed SAP to make its Select events feel more exclusive and inclusive, all at the same time.

Working with its agency partner George P. Johnson, SAP set out to combine the most successful elements of its entire events portfolio into a single experience that could be dropped in global cities around the world. SAP Select, which launched in Beijing and ended in Berlin, used unique branding architecture, moving away from its standard SAP branding and transforming *all* of the event's conference spaces into fully branded experiences. For instance, while you may have been checking into the China World Summit Hotel in Beijing or the Ritz-Carlton or Marriott in Berlin, for three days you were actually checking into the "SAP Select Hotel."

The brand leveraged the properties in unique ways, such as converting guest sleeping rooms into offices for one-on-one meetings with customers and converting restaurants and bars into branded experiences and workspaces. Each site featured artistic experiences as well. In Berlin, for example, the atrium of the Marriott was transformed during the evenings into an "aquarium" with aerial dancers performing overhead, sea creatures floating through the six-story atrium, and performances on open balconies. "Showcases" were integrated into the venues, too, to demonstrate to customers how SAP solutions support popular sports such as McLaren's F1 Racing Team, the German National Soccer Team, Women's Tennis, Professional Golf, and Extreme Sailing.

As for the content, SAP monitored registrations and, where the company's marketers saw increases in various industries or lines of business, they added thought leadership content to address these people specifically. Taking it a step further, SAP gave attendees room to breathe, with only half of their schedules pre-booked, allowing them plenty of flexibility to network.

Thanks to this strategy, SAP Select's average booked/won business per company was 7.4 times greater than in its previous SAPHIRE NOW model. ROI increased 345 percent in China and 246 percent in Europe. The program took *experience customization* to a new level by designing content around who was attending the show, and it tapped into a growing trend by "taking over" all of its attendees' on-site touch points and turning them into branded engagements. The revised strategy also embedded more flexibility into the schedule so there was ample time for networking.

From a measurement point of view, there are two important factors to consider:

1. SAP Select was designed to replace the "one size fits all" model of the SAPPHIRE NOW program that had been previously produced in each location. Measurements are based on how this new format performed versus the SAPPHIRE NOW performances.
2. SAP Select was produced in each location at 25 percent of the expense of the SAPPHIRE NOW format.

Given that, SAP Select exceeded all projections and expectations:

- Pipeline acceleration was 2.4 times greater than the SAPPHIRE NOW model.
- Average booked/won business per company was 7.4 times greater than the SAPPHIRE NOW model.
- Average pipeline value of an attendee was 4.8 times that of SAPPHIRE NOW attendees.
- The Net Promoter Score of SAP as a company increased 207 percent, the highest value ever tracked on any event format. As a comparison, in Europe, this was a 714 percent increase versus the previous SAP-PHIRE NOW Net Promoter Scores.
- Sixty-five percent of the attendees at SAP Select left stating that as a result of the event they would change the plan on how to implement SAP solutions, products, or services
- Ninety percent of responders agreed that SAP "Is Going in the Right Direction" with a 13-point lift in "Very Accurate," an 86 percent increase.
- Nine out of 10 post-event survey responders believed SAP "Is an Innovative Company," a 26 percent gain from the pre-event survey response, and a dramatic reduction in negative and neutral responses by greater than two-thirds.
- Within 30 days of the event in Europe, 23 percent of the attended pipeline converted to Booked/Won.

These results support our recommendation in Chapter 7 to create performance benchmarks that you can use across your events to document performance over time.

RELATABLE

Experiences have to relate to the people having them in order for them to be memorable and sharable. In other words, they have to align with the wants, needs, desires, and aspirations of the target audience. And they have to be crafted in a way that feels authentic and natural, and not contrived by a company's marketing department.

Jim Beam "Makes History"

Beam Suntory's Jim Beam whiskey brand was looking for a way to reinforce its 219-year heritage while inviting new bourbon drinkers to the brand family. The solution was a Bourbon Bar experience that offered consumers a highly consultative brand interaction rich with personalized recommendations and ideas they could use on the spot. This program created a highly personalized engagement platform that used consumer insights to create relevant and contextual purchase recommendations. A customized high-tech component rewarded consumers instantly for sharing their personal data.

The premise of the campaign, which was created with agency partner Geometry Global, was that as more Americans are filling their plates with farm-to-table produce and free-range meat, they're also washing it down with small-batch, organic, and locally made bourbons. Jim Beam tackled this trend head on with a Millennial-male-targeted, in-store sampling campaign that reinforced the brand's story in an intimate one-on-one setting.

The brand's off-premise activation strategy had three key objectives: (1) get whiskey-drinking guys ages 21 to 29 to reconsider and purchase Jim Beam; (2) amplify the effort by connecting it to the Jim Beam "Make History" platform; and (3) extend the conversation through an integrated CRM program. Jim Beam started the conversation through a series of pop-up sampling events in more than 14 markets that transformed a trip to the local liquor store into a visit with your favorite bartender.

Inside stores, brand ambassadors invited shoppers to pull up a stool and join them at the Bourbon Bar for a proper bourbon tasting. Through casual conversation, staffers identified the occasion consumers were shopping for and then made a personalized Jim Beam brand recommendation that would complement their plans. The signature Jim Beam cocktail (prepared on-site) further elevated the encounter by going beyond the usual "plus-one" drink recipe (e.g., whiskey and cola), reintroducing them to an American classic in a new way. With three Jim Beam variants and a signature Jim Beam cocktail on hand, the brand's "bartenders" had plenty of options to familiarize consumers with the brand, arm them with valuable bourbon education, and bring new bourbon drinkers into the category.

Adding to the experience, participants were invited to join the online "I'm Beam" program and instantly print a customized Jim Beam White label on-site. Using a mobile app, consumers inserted their own pictures into the label alongside the other woodcut portraits of the Jim Beam family. Staffers printed and gifted the personalized label, marking the consumer's "initiation" into the Beam family.

The program generated 68 percent growth in event sales year-over-year. Emily Carpin, Beam's senior brand activation manager, called it "one of the most successful off-premise programs in the history of Beam."

Ford Creates a Movement

Ford Motor Company and its agency partners Team Detroit and Match Action devised a clever way to personalize a campaign for its Fiesta automobiles, targeting the Millennial audience by tapping into the demographic's affinity for creating and consuming user-generated content.

The Fiesta Movement had launched the compact vehicle to great success, but sales had slipped 22 percent in the year before the brand launched this sequel. Ford hoped to reverse the decline by bringing Millennial drivers into the fold. The company set out to find 100 influencers to "own" its campaign, and a Fiesta, for six months. Millennials did not see Ford as the brand for them, so the selection of influencers to receive a car was critical. After Ford gave each "Fiesta Agent" a car, gas card, camera, insurance, and a list of missions, they set out to show off the Fiesta's moves. The Agents created thousands of intriguing and entertaining pieces of content, all communicating the car's personality and how it could be part of Millennials' active and urban lifestyles. Ford amplified the best Agent content across digital, print, broadcast, and outdoor media, making it Ford's first ever 100 percent user-generated campaign.

One of Ford's core objectives was to generate 310,000 "build and price" actions online during the seven-month campaign. Consumers who took the time to go through the build and price process are considered key leads because of the time spent with a vehicle, and because they're more likely to request a quote or dealer contact. Ford had enough substantial history on this metric to establish an objective with confidence that it would correlate to sales performance.

The Fiesta Movement took the car to a record high in sales and captured more of the target audience than any other car in its class. Among Millennials, the Fiesta made up 30 percent of car sales, which demonstrates the power in this campaign of using Millennials to reach other Millennials. Choosing brand advocates that the target audience could relate to was critical in creating engagement among this elusive group. The agents created more than 14,000 pieces of content, with many millions of YouTube views, photo views, and Twitter and Facebook exposures. And to top it off, nearly 450,000 consumers built and priced Fiestas during the campaign—140,000 more than goal.

Jack Daniel's Customers Build a Bar

Another relatable example from the spirits category is a unique campaign from Australia in which Jack Daniel's summoned the help of whiskey drinkers to create the world's first crowdsourced bar. The premise was simple: help build a bar, get free whiskey.

Jack Daniel's was losing prominence among its standard middle-aged, blue-collar customers in the face of emerging craft whiskey brands. To reconnect, engage, and reward Jack Daniel's loyalists, the brand created "The Bar That Jack Built," an experiential program catering to the typical Jack Daniel's drinker—one who values authentic things that exist in the real world and who enjoys being a "doer" by working with his hands.

With these Jack loyalists in mind, the brand launched a six-week social media and word-of-mouth effort, offering consumers a chance to work for Jack, literally, by building a bar to celebrate Jack Daniel's 148th birthday. The brand put the word out, asking for materials, labor, time, and expertise. Before long, laborers, sculptors, welders, fabricators, painters, artists, electricians, and a variety of other professionals had been recruited—all in exchange for whiskey. The more materials, time, or expertise they volunteered, the more Jack Daniel's they received, along with a ticket to a huge birthday bash to be held inside the finished product: the world's first crowdsourced bar.

Everything was crowdsourced, from the bar itself to the workforce, collection trucks, event invitations, entertainment on the night of the bar's opening, and even three of the campaign's six content films. The brand racked up 10,000 new Facebook fans, increased engagement by 178 percent, and received $178,000 worth of donated time, materials, and expertise—all for the cost of 268 bottles of whiskey.

PERSONAL

One of the biggest conundrums marketers face when building an experiential program is how to personalize an experience while also reaching as many of the right people as possible. This can be accomplished in a number of ways. Technology such as RFID and other identification methods that link to registration information and/or preferences can trigger delivery of, or access to, customized content or entertainment. Providing tools for participants to have a hand in crafting the experience is another great way to personalize an otherwise broad-reach program.

Google Uses Tech to Allow Personal Journeys

For its Think Event series, Google created a customized event experience that amplified on-stage programming and entertained clients in a uniquely Google way. Using a series of custom-built experiential solutions, all attendees were taken on a personalized "Think Event Journey" that felt as though the event was designed specifically for them, and only them.

There were numerous standout components involved in creating this custom experience, all of which were made possible by RFID registration. The first was the Think Event Registration app, which collected client-specific information regarding favorite hobbies (sports, movies and TV, fashion and beauty, cars, food, and tech), as well as their favorite beverages. This collection process led to the next component of custom activation—the Personalized YouTube Ads Leaderboard.

An attendee would walk up to a touch screen, scan his or her badge to check in, and upon doing so, see a curated list of the year's top YouTube ads based on the hobbies he or she had expressed interest in during registration. Google hosted 955 clients at five events, delivered 803 pieces of "Think with Google" content to clients' inboxes, streamed an average of 850 YouTube ads per event via the Personalized Ad Leaderboard, and served more than 250 drinks per event using the Google Express Bar.

Verizon Creates an NFL Fan Playbook

Wireless carrier Verizon leveraged its sponsorship of the NFL as a platform to translate its national marketing message into a personalized experience for football fans as a way to create awareness and trial of the carrier's technology solutions. Verizon conceptualized its activation experiences around what football fans would enjoy, then seeded the brand message within a customized user journey. By deploying a variety of personalized technology experiences, the brand empowered participants to self-discover their way through a new-age technology (and NFL) world.

As a major sponsor of the NFL, Verizon knew it had to stand out among the clutter of brands vying for attention as football fans ramped up for the Super Bowl. Their solution was simple: Make every participant feel like a special guest. To achieve this, the brand transformed New York City's Bryant Park into a 15,000-square-foot Power House showcase of personalized, interactive technology experiences for Super Bowl fans that tapped into their passion for football and the NFL. The technology and innovation experiences inside the space were designed to shift Verizon's brand perception from a mobile service provider to a leading technology innovator.

Personalization began as soon as consumers walked in the door. With the help of biometric scan technology, participants created customized profiles with their fingerprints, photos, and personal information. Fans then simply scanned into each Power House experience to personalize their interactions. Twelve unique touchpoints provided participants with a variety of experiences. Each fan had the opportunity to learn about NFL Mobile through "live" and personalized chats with NFL players; create a customized timeline of his life featuring the most iconic moments in NFL, pop culture, and tech history; play with an interactive wall showcasing many of Verizon's Powerful Answers stories; learn about the benefits of a Verizon-connected life through a unique 270-degree projection mapping experience; and embark on other tech-centric adventures.

Content generated within the space was posted on the Wall of Fame and online (made possible by Verizon's Cloud services). To wrap up the experience, as visitors exited the space, the brand offered complimentary phone charging via biometric scanning, as well as a pair of texting gloves to help fight the bitter cold outside.

Verizon achieved results that will likely serve as benchmarks for future Super Bowl activations. The experience engaged 29,000 visitors over the course of five days, earning an average dwell time of 25 minutes per guest.

TARGETABLE

Experiences have evolved from attracting huge crowds to engaging with specific target groups who self-select their participation. More marketers are shifting to smaller-scale experiences—often within large-scale campaigns—that engage highly defined target groups (or several groups) and offer up tailored content that amplifies and activates the other Experiential Pillars.

Red Bull Goes to College

Millennials are an elusive target that many consumer marketers are anxious to reach. Millennials are digital natives, and they seek meaning from the relationships they have with employers and the companies whose products and services they purchase and use.

The back-to-school season presents an enticing opportunity for brands to target this demographic. It also presents a challenge for brands looking to gain exclusive access and scale for their experiences. Red Bull decided to go straight into the classroom and infiltrate buildings with relevant surprise-and-delight experiences centered on helping students prepare for the semester.

Working with its agency partner Fluent, Red Bull targeted Boston, home to scores of college and universities, where teams of student representatives took to classrooms across nine campuses on the first days of classes, placing cans of Red Bull Edition along with a campus-specific

Red Bull "Syllabus Hack." Each campus's syllabus included a narrative on how to capitalize on unique campus traditions and make the most of the first semester. The student reps created target lists of classrooms on their respective campuses to deliver the cans and syllabi, ranging from large auditoriums to smaller intimate settings.

Each syllabus contained the Red Bull Boston Twitter and Instagram handles along with a program hashtag to encourage dialog on social platforms. The second phase of the program involved kick-off events on campus. Red Bull professional action sports athlete Thomas Oehler performed demonstrations for and with students, often making them obstacles for his stunts. On top of these engagements, Red Bull hosted a socially driven scavenger hunt involving Red Bull three-pack products. Thanks to the engagement strategy, Red Bull enjoyed 1.5 million-plus media impressions, with 107 Boston classrooms receiving 15,336 "Syllabus Hacks."

The syllabus hack demonstrated the brand's rebellious and whimsical nature, while large-scale athlete demonstrations exemplified the extreme, daredevil mentality often associated with Red Bull, and finally the party and social scavenger hunt activations brought surprise and delight to students during a time when they are keen to create associations around unique experiences.

The entire program was based on the insight that the true "back to school" period is more than just a marketing period, but one of the more elite "big moments" among college students that Red Bull could use to engage with this audience in an authentic way . . . all while celebrating one of the most important rites of passage in their college careers. In addition to the students who witnessed the athlete demonstrations in person, hundreds of thousands more absorbed the experience through media outlets. Additionally, through the student network, Red Bull brand presence quadrupled on Boston campuses.

Lexus Targets New Segment with Secret Events

When Lexus decided to aim for a slightly younger audience, the brand set out to show that a Lexus is the best way to pair luxury with a unique statement of taste and refinement. The brand used market research to determine that its target consumers—the Generation X and Y demographics—love fine dining; they want to eat at the best restaurants and have the best experiences. So Lexus worked with agency partner Team One and enlisted with *Los Angeles Magazine,* to create a fine-dining partnership that offered up exclusive dining experiences to Lexus guests.

The magazine's readership matched the audience Lexus wanted to reach, with high disposable income and influence. To reach these discerning customers, the campaign began with print ads in the publication and a call to enter an online sweepstakes, and culminated in a full editorial takeover, with run-of-site media and an eblast promoting the main events: two pop-up dinner experiences.

Lexus's target consumers love exclusive and "secret" venues and events, so Lexus used the magazine's reach to inform readers about some of the best ones in the city, while inviting them into area dealerships and enticing them to enter the online sweepstakes for invitations to the hidden dinners. The Los Angeles Lexus Dealers Association worked with *Los Angeles Magazine's* subscriber list to invite guests to the two pop-up dinners and two of the secret venues that had been featured in the custom issue.

All guests were required to RSVP, but did not know the location of the events until the day prior. In the end, the media blitz and events resulted in 10 new vehicle sales for Lexus, and millions of impressions, unique web visits, and social media returns.

CONNECTABLE

Experiences need multiple points of connection—among participants as well as with other elements of the marketing mix. It is only with these connections that the true value of an experiential strategy can be realized to its maximum potential. The experience should be the hub that fuels, amplifies, and optimizes your other marketing and media platforms. Nowhere is the idea of "connectedness" more visible than in the "digital-plus-live" strides that the leading proponents of experiential marketing have pioneered and continue to explore.

Microsoft Uses Online Strategy to Extend Live Engagement

The Worldwide Partner Conference (WPC) is the premier annual event for Microsoft's partner network. Through keynote addresses, educational sessions, and networking events, Microsoft's business partners have the opportunity to hear the company's vision for the year, learn industry trends and best practices, meet with Microsoft representatives, and—hopefully—form profitable connections with one another.

Microsoft's event team wanted to augment the in-person experience with a digital strategy that would connect attendees to the show's content and to each other earlier and more frequently before, during, and after the event. To accomplish this, Microsoft's event marketing team employed a combination of social media and digital engagement strategies. The most complex of these was a custom social media network called Connect, which enabled partners to get a jump-start on networking by enabling them to connect digitally with one another well before the conference opened.

It also allowed them to plan ahead and build their schedules. This way, attendees walked into WPC with their schedules planned and with potentially profitable relationships already germinating. After the conference, Connect was where partners could access session resources, including viewing on-demand videos. The brand knew that attendees wanted to have information at their fingertips, so the features and functionality of Connect came through the mobile app. In addition to the Connect features, Microsoft also leveraged more traditional social channels, including Facebook and Twitter, which the brand used to engage in conversations with attendees in real time.

A team of four used a social listening tool to monitor and respond immediately to attendee issues, whether that response was a simple thank you or a troubleshooting escalation. One of the most important parts of WPC is the Vision Keynotes, so the brand streamed the keynotes live on its website, DigitalWPC. In addition to the live streaming, Microsoft brought the keynote experience to the digital world through live tweeting of quotes, key announcements, and posting live interviews from the press box. For an exciting technological touch, the brand brought online conversations to the real world with a Live Wall that displayed a living infographic of social feeds, statistics, and presentation decks. In the end,

Microsoft's digital additions helped transform its annual conference into a year-round conversation capped off with a better-organized and more networking-friendly live experience.

Connect brought together vendors, tools, and features into one seamless experience for attendees to help augment their event experience. The app brought more than 8,000 users into the fold, and almost 90,000 total app opens. Thanks to the brand's careful social management, it increased its Twitter reach by more than one million over the year before, 61 percent of messages sent by the brand team were retweeted, and mentions increased 219 percent. In addition, the live streaming had three times the viewership for the Vision Keynotes over the prior event, with more than 20,000 viewers from more than 100 countries.

Coke Scores Big with Banner Experience

As an official sponsor of the FIFA World Cup, Coca-Cola's marketing campaign around the FIFA World Cup Brazil was built on the idea of making the World Cup the *World's* Cup—transforming it into the most inclusive, engaging, and participatory FIFA World Cup flag presentation experience to date.

Coke's objective was to harness the power of soccer to bring together people from different races, places, classes, and creeds—all leading up to the FIFA World Cup. To meet this objective, Coke's solution was the Happiness Flag, the world's largest digitally produced photomosaic flag. It's a custom in soccer to present flags on the field or in the stands, typically representative of the teams or nations about to play.

The idea for the Happiness Flag was to create a flag to unveil on the pitch that was representative of everybody, regardless of team or country. With agency partner Ignition, Coke invited soccer fans around the world to submit pictures of themselves through social media, e-mail, and the Happiness Flag website. Local artists designed and painted a beautiful canvas in collaboration with Coca-Cola, and once the canvas was completed it was digitized, and all of the fan-submitted images were then put together as a massive photomosaic that was later unveiled on the pitch before the opening match in São Paulo, Brazil, in front of a global audience.

The Happiness Flag provided an easy way for users to engage—all they had to do was submit their pictures by sharing them on social media. The brand capitalized on the ease and popularity of familiar social channels and hashtags, and already-common consumer actions, like selfies. Overall, Coke collected images from 207 different countries around the world—every single country that Coca-Cola is sold in.

After the opening soccer match, the flag was uploaded to the Happiness Flag website, allowing consumers to zoom in, find their pictures, and share them again on their social channels, taking the campaign full circle. The physical flag was then leveraged as event décor in subsequent Coca-Cola FIFA World Cup hospitality events. Later, pieces of the flag were actually given back to participating markets after the tournament as a FIFA World Cup souvenir.

Through Facebook, Twitter, Instagram, and the Happiness Flag website, the brand was able to leverage technology to reach consumers and gain participation all around the world. The Happiness Flag was composed of more than 3.5 million images and 223,206 fan photos, all voluntarily submitted by consumers. The flag itself was printed on 192 nylon fabric panels; after 29 straight days of printing, the final product was 32,453 square feet.

The Opening Ceremony received about 2.8 billion viewers, meaning that the Happiness Flag unveiling created almost three billion impressions worldwide. And the campaign continued to thrive off of social sharing. After the unveiling, 22,000 posts generated an estimated 703 million impressions online. Coca-Cola's real-time Happiness Flag tweets generated more than three million retweets, and the digital flag on the Happiness Flag website generated upwards of 1.5 million views, just during the game.

FLEXIBLE

A one-size-fits-all strategy may be effective in reaching an audience, but experiential marketing pros understand that building flexibility into their campaigns allows them to capitalize on opportunities to reach tangential markets or locations that might otherwise be missed. Experiential programs that can be scaled up or down allow marketers to optimize their investments by extending reach and engagement, often for little or nominal additional cost.

BASF Extends Trade Show Presence

BASF wanted to showcase its portfolio of residential construction products that can be used for sustainable buildings. So at the International Builders' Show in Las Vegas, they worked with partner Impact Unlimited to extend BASF's floor presence into the parking lot outside the convention center. There, the company erected a full-scale home, complete with landscaping and decking, shown in both its construction and finished phases, to drive adoption of BASF products. Invited visitors could tour the company's net-zero-energy home and educate themselves on the products available to build more energy-efficient homes.

A hostess greeted visitors, set them up with RFID bracelets, and then sent small groups on guided tours. There were 12 stops throughout the experience where the guides highlighted products and used iPads that allowed them to activate monitors to play videos or cue lights that focused the attention of visitors on specific solutions. As the visitors identified products of interest, they tapped their RFID wristbands at tap stations, and information was automatically e-mailed to them. BASF collected valuable information about product preferences and customized additional digital information tailored to the individual visitors' interests. A virtual tour of the home—every room, every product stop, and every video—was made available after the show.

The strategy was a clever way to take advantage of the targeted audience attending the trade show in a way that allowed BASF to create targeted engagements away from the competitive clutter of the trade show floor (where the company also had a large exhibit). Over the course of the three-day trade show, more than 1,700 toured the show home, representing a 20 percent increase over the previous year's count.

L'Oréal Customizes for College Campuses

L'Oréal originally targeted its Healthy Look Crème Gloss product toward a mature female audience in search of a premium, non-permanent hair coloring solution. But sales data showed that the brand might be missing out on a substantial opportunity among a younger audience more apt to experiment with color on a regular basis, and who are among a growing segment of "home dyers." So the brand launched "Play with Color," a collegiate marketing campaign that involved 70 female student influencers who engaged their classmates across 35 campuses nationwide.

The campaign, as we discussed in Chapter 3, was adapted to each campus and featured hair coloring parties with sororities, fashion clubs, and dorm and apartment complexes, as well as direct outreach through peer-to-peer communication and networks. Coupon distribution and social media contests incentivized students to try the product. Guerrilla marketing tactics allowed women to "play with color" without any true physical transformation through mirror clings in high-traffic women's bathrooms, which included calls to action that drove social media engagement.

Ultimately, these college Millennials were introduced to a new "accessory"—their hair—as something they could play with as part of a daily routine to change up their style and look on any given day. They felt comfortable sharing the experience with peers and on social media, and with the proper education on the product, most felt comfortable giving it a try.

L'Oréal's program engaged 35,280 Healthy Look Crème Gloss coloring participants; 12,058 female students tried the Healthy Look product in groups through hair coloring parties (as well as the before/after hair color contests). There were 310,400 L'Orèal Healthy Look Crème Gloss coupons distributed, and the effort earned a nearly 4 percent redemption rate.

Pepsi Hypes Halftime Off the Field

Pepsi took its sponsorship of the biggest media event of the year, the Super Bowl halftime show, and set out to make it even bigger by using a series of events to build excitement around the show and make it the most-viewed television event in history. The "Get Hyped for Halftime" program, created with agency partner Motive, shrewdly tapped into one of the hottest trends in experiential marketing: taking huge cultural events and anchoring them to hyper-local activations.

Pepsi's sponsorship of the Super Bowl XLVIII Halftime Show featuring Bruno Mars was not going to be anything less than spectacular. But an epic-style live show is only as good as its audience, and Pepsi knew that that audience needed to be bigger than any other. The concept was to flood the country with amazing experiences and event activations that would either unexpectedly "halftime" a key moment in a consumer's day or help fans "get hyped" for the Super Bowl performance with an incredible public happening.

The brand started months ahead of time by "halftiming" large and small events, from the Grammy Awards to a retirement home Bingo night. The real hyping started in a truly unlikely place, however: Milligan, Nebraska. The brand transformed this tiny town into a fan destination, surprising and delighting locals all over the state. On a Thursday morning one week, residents suddenly found Pepsi vending machines all over town. Each one gave out free sodas, and every can had a teaser sticker hinting at a secret event on that Saturday night. The word spread. Local radio and news grabbed the story, but national media was gobbling it up almost as fast, while word-of-mouth ran like wildfire from person to person all over the Midwest. By event night, hundreds of people were gathered in the center of town on nothing but a hunch that something cool was about to happen. When the lights went out on Main Street, the crowd held its breath. When singer Lee Brice took the stage, the crowd went nuts. Pepsi staged three of these types of surprise events, each one progressively bigger, leading up to the big Super Bowl show.

The campaign helped drive awareness for what became the most-viewed Super Bowl Halftime Show of all time, which would have been enough for some brands, but Pepsi also scored 300 million media impressions, 12,000 on-site engagements, and a viral YouTube video with more than 1.2 million views.

ENGAGEABLE

Experiences are not spectator sports. In order to activate the other Experiential Pillars and deliver the true promise of experiential marketing, your experiences must stimulate the active involvement of your target audience. Engagement occurs when participants perceive they are going to receive value in exchange for the time they invest with your brand. Value can be in the form of a discount coupon, but financial incentives rarely motivate anyone to engage in a meaningful way. Rather, perceived value increases in direct proportion to how well your experience fulfills the needs and desires of your target audience. When creating an experiential marketing program, ask yourself these questions:

- How will the experience connect with my target audience?
- How will the experience inspire my target audience to take a specific action?
- How will the experience allow my target audience to explore, discover, and learn about my product or service, and how will using it improve their lives?
- How will the experience deliver on my brand promise?
- Will the experience stimulate my audience to share their experience with their friends?
- Have I provided tools to facilitate sharing?

Your engagement strategy is the key to ensuring that your campaign resonates and delivers results. Take the time to ensure that what you are creating provides as much perceived value (or more) to the participants as you want in financial return.

Air Force Connects with Career Seekers

The Air Force Recruiting Service created a mobile Performance Lab, which is a personalized mobile tour designed to highlight career opportunities to potential recruits. The Lab visits air shows, schools, and other events, where the engagement begins at registration with RFID wristbands that capture attendee data and track and compute their scores throughout five on-site interactives. Once inside the lab, which is housed in a 53-foot expandable trailer, attendees compete with each other via a series of challenges and interactive games that test spatial and mechanical skills, dexterity, situational awareness, logic and reasoning, and physical strength. The experience begins with high-tech puzzles offered on touch screen monitors offering two-minute quizzes.

From there, participants move to the Oculus Rift activation, which represents the largest mixed use of technology in an Air Force recruiting experience—combining Kinect 2 motion sensory tech and Oculus Rift VR. Attendees are strapped into a cockpit equipped with rumble packs to mimic the vibrations of a jet, a joystick, and an Oculus headset. The 360-degree skills blind course has participants flying an F-35 and following a wingman through a canyon. The goal is to navigate through graphical rings and be as accurate as possible.

Outside the trailer, attendees take part in a Kinect 2–based physical challenge in which they choose Special Ops airmen or airwomen and compete against them, virtually, to see how many pull-ups they can do in 30 seconds. Throughout the experience, the participants' scores were displayed on an on-site leaderboard.

The final experience is the interactive career center featuring a wall of 30 removable iPads that each displays information on an Air Force career. The center is helping the Air Force reinforce the marketing messaging that its branch of the armed services offers more than 150 careers. The Air Force is able to assess qualified leads through its digital data capture program and, from there, recruiters are able to connect with attendees in real time and answer any questions they might have about the Air Force or a specific career field.

"It's been a huge hit since our launch," Major Jacob Chisolm, chief-event branch at the Air Force told us. "We're trying to reach those with a particularly heightened interest in science, technology, engineering, and math, and we've made a concerted effort to target folks interested in special operations through the experiences in the footprint."

As this book went to press, the tour had attracted more than 3,870 registrants with an average of 61 qualified leads per event. Visitors on average were spending 15 minutes in the experience. Agencies included: GSD&M (activation); Craftsmen Industries (build); FISH; Reel FX (production); Next Marketing (tour operations).

Google Cracks the Code for Engagement

Google targeted the next demographic to rise up the ranks—Gen Z, a native digital audience—with the kind of participatory and hyper-digital experiences they crave. This program tapped into a hot-button topic in a way that felt real, and seamlessly integrated its online program with a traditional TV broadcast as a way to generate reach and greater exposure.

As we discussed in Chapter 3, Google created engagement around the topic of women in technology with a program that was both authentic to the brand and meaningful to its female audience. Less than 1 percent of girls express interest in majoring in computer science in college. Yet the tech industry is growing faster than any other industry. To champion this issue and be sure that the future of tech includes perspectives from women, Google created Made with Code, an initiative to inspire girls to try coding and be inspired to pursue their dream careers.

Google wanted a big stage from which to launch this initiative and engage girls in the campaign, so it partnered with the National Park Foundation and National Park Service to let girls bring the National Tree Lighting holiday ceremony to life through code. On a Made with Code website, girls could use an introductory coding experience to design the colors, patterns, and animation of the lights on one of 56 state and territory trees outside of the White House.

Each girl's completed design was sent to Washington D.C., and incorporated into her selected state tree lighting scheme. She then received the date and the time of when her design would light up. The 56 coded trees lit up alongside the National Holiday Tree at the annual televised event, each covered in 900 interactive LED lights that responded to the girls' designs, but also coordinated to light up in sync with one another. More than 2,000 people, including many of the girls who coded trees, were in attendance along with the First Family, hosts Tom Hanks and Rita Wilson, and famous musical guests.

In addition to the event's ability to engage audiences in a Google cause, the brand announced a $50 million commitment over three years to support an ecosystem of nonprofit partners who are exposing girls to computer science. In one month, with no paid media, more than one million digital trees were coded. The project received unanimous praise from mainstream press, such as *The New York Times*, *Washington Post*, *Seventeen*, and *Mashable*.

BELIEVABLE

Marketers can't fake authenticity. The experience must emanate from the brand heritage or the brand story, and if your brand doesn't have one (or doesn't have a compelling one), then your first step is to find and/or build one. People today want to know what the companies with whom they do business stand for, so it is imperative that your experiences be aligned with your brand story and brand promise. Anything less than real, authentic alignment will dampen your ability to inspire real engagement, let alone create or enhance strong customer relationships.

Activision Gets Real with Call of Duty Experience

Call of Duty: XP immersed fans in Modern Warfare 3, the latest game in the popular Activision Call of Duty series. The result was epic in scope and authentic in execution, as it literally brought the game to life and set a new bar for experiential fan-based events, delivering blockbuster sales and brand results to the tune of $775 million—in just the first five days—and eventually becoming the first entertainment launch in history to reach $1 billion. As if that weren't enough, the program generated 2.4 billion impressions and $21.5 million in earned media coverage.

The two-day, open-air, on-the-ground experience pitted Call of Duty fans against each other in real-life contests and electronic gameplay. Participants fought their way through an obstacle course, pelted one another in paintball fights, and whizzed above the action on military-style zip lines, battling it out to become king of the hill. More than 6,000 fans paid to attend the live event, which took place on a 16-acre compound that mimicked the landscapes in the iconic game franchise in the urban confines of Los Angeles over Labor Day weekend. Along with the press, celebrities, marketing partners, and military veterans, fans participated in the world premiere of Modern Warfare 3 three months before it hit retail shelves.

A series of real-world Call of Duty action experiences and gaming competitions supported the epic reveal of the new game, along with a $1 million Call of Duty tournament—the largest prize purse in gaming history—offered by Activision and the event's lead sponsor, Microsoft

Xbox 360. Fans qualified for the tournament prior to the event in regional promotions and competitions. Others qualified onsite. All this came at a price of $150 for tickets, which Activision donated to the Call of Duty Endowment, a nonprofit corporation that helps veterans transition to civilian life, find work, and establish careers. For their money, fans supported a worthy cause and took a deep dive into the action in and around the Hughes Cargo Building in Playa Vista, California, the site where Howard Hughes built his "Spruce Goose" plane in 1947.

Besides the life-sized game-play areas from the Black Ops edition, the experience included a driving course designed by brand partner Jeep, an overhead zip line, and re-creations of Burger Town and Juggernaut Sumo (both from the game), not to mention the 7,600 Xbox gaming stations provided by Microsoft. Keynote speeches, press conferences, discussion panels, and Q&A sessions with Call of Duty developers offered a behind-the-scenes look at the development process and the people responsible for creating the game and the franchise. Inside a giant airplane hangar, a Call of Duty armory displayed military weapons and combat gear and Call of Duty concept art and research, and recounted the history of one of the most celebrated franchises in gaming. A merchandise shop sold custom T-shirts and other goods. Roving game avatars and photo ops for social network sharing added to the fun.

At a time when marketers were focused on pushing live events online, Activision did just the opposite. With an inherently all-digital product— a pre-built virtual environment on Microsoft's Xbox Live—Activision *could* have created an all-digital event. The tech-friendly fans of the game probably wouldn't have minded. But instead it executed an experience that transported its digital audience into a physical rendition of the game, one that matched its size, scale, and sophistication on all fronts.

A solid online component with social media and constant updates, the result was an event that reached far beyond those 6,000 attendees and touched millions. Video game marketers are continually challenged with selling new products to the savvy gamer audience, often without their having seen the game. Because sales rely on pre-orders and support by early adopters in the gaming community, Activision knew it had to bring Modern Warfare 3 to a new level. Activision also realized early on that with the changing media landscape, consumers have become just as powerful as traditional media when it comes to promoting a new product. So with the help of experiential agency NCompass International, Activision transformed what had previously been a media-only event into one that would involve consumers and harness the power of their influence.

"We wanted to do something that had never been done before," said Byron Beede, senior director of marketing for Call of Duty at Activision. "We wanted to treat our fans, take the multiplayer reveal and make it a fan experience, not just a gaming experience. Then it grew into a passion project."

Its target audience was primarily current fans of the Call of Duty franchise, a devoted but discerning community of 30 million plus. Other entertainment, games, and sports enthusiasts not presently engaged with the brand comprised a secondary target, followed by fans and consumers of competitive gaming titles. The brand also set its sights on a broad spectrum of global press, including current events, financial, lifestyle, gaming, sports, technology, and entertainment writers, along with mainstream and niche social media influencers. The result was an epic, authentic, blockbuster brand experience that for three days literally brought the game to life in a 270,000-square-foot raw space that included two massive airplane hangars and exuded the feeling of a military installation. The place looked and felt as though the government had come in and set up a field base of forward operations, especially from the outside. Inside, the traditional military imagery gave some room up to the idealized video game look, but kept the COD feel. "For Call of Duty, it's always about trying to do something awe-inspiring," says Beede.

AMEX Celebrates Golf Connection

Since 2007, American Express has been activating at the U.S. Open Golf Championship. The company's goal has been to provide card members and prospects with benefits that make their U.S. Open experience even more memorable. As with many of its other sports sponsorships, American Express wanted to create an on-site experience that allowed card members and prospects to digitally capture their experience in a highly relevant, shareable, and personalized way—connecting to their passion for watching, learning about, and playing golf.

American Express's activation at Pinehurst, home of the 2014 U.S. Open, was as smooth as a well-honed golf swing that propelled the financial services company straight into the digital age with the MyOpen Pass RFID Experience. The activation came to life in the 20,000-square-foot U.S. Open American Express Fan Experience where fans registered for a MyOpen RFID wristband. By adding their names and e-mail addresses, they immediately received a personalized e-mail containing the MyOpen dashboard, where all of the day's content would ultimately be stored. After donning the wristbands, they explored the activation, which featured swing analysis hitting bays outfitted with the latest technology.

A Rally Cam captured 180-degree GIF photos, a Pro Cam offered an augmented reality experience with pro player Sloane Stephens, and an interactive PERCH table showcased the game's historic fashion and equipment. Fans could experience each element as many times as they wished. All was saved in a carousel of content on their MyOpen dashboard. More than 200,000 fans entered the Fan Experience, and 30,000 registered for the wristbands. MyOpen saw more than 80,000 interactions. The brand achieved more than 380 million total impressions, and its perception by way of social sentiment saw positive increases, up 7 percent year over year.

The campaigns we've highlighted in this chapter represent companies in different industries, with budgets large and small, trying to reach numerous target audiences. The one thing they have in common is their understanding of how to connect the 11 Experiential Pillars to deliver programs that create measurable business impact, create and enhance relationships, and deliver on their brand promises. Incorporating some of these pillars into your marketing campaigns can potentially enhance your results, but incorporating all of them is essential to achieving the strongest business impact that experiential marketing can deliver.

REFERENCE

EMI/Freeman XP. *The viral impact of events*. Norwalk, CT: Event Marketing Institute, February 2015.

Chapter Five   Digital Plus Live

The integration of social media and technology into experiential marketing strategies provides brands around the world with a powerful engagement platform. Gone are the days when experiences lived for mere minutes, hours, or days. When combined with interactive technology and digital channels, brand experiences can live on for much longer periods of time. Marketers also have the capability to use social media to amplify an engagement to thousands or even millions of people who aren't attending a live experience. And those attendees, when given share-worthy experiences, will create and share content themselves—effectively self-amplifying their experiences for a brand.

Marketers continue to refine how they leverage social media and technology across live experiences. Across both business-to-consumer and business-to-business brands, an experiential digital strategy has become critical to the success of programs. Properly fused online and offline engagements share four Digital Live Stems:

Stem 1. Extended Communications. Marketers are using technology and social media to extend brand experiences. Digital tools and elements allow dialogs to begin early, stay constant during a live experience, and then continue.

Stem 2. Amplified Engagements. Singular or collective social media activation married with interactive technologies allows brands to multiply experiences directed at hundreds or thousands of people to millions of others.

Stem 3. Shared and Shareable Moments. Interactive technologies and use of social media allow marketers to create experiences that are shared *and* shareable. By shared, we refer to elements of the experience that attendees engage as shared moments together. And by shareable, we refer to the increased movement among attendees to capture and share content from experiences with others.

Stem 4. Customized Interactions. The best engagements are the ones experienced in completely different ways by the target audience. Social media and technology allow marketers to craft different experiences for every member of an audience. No two attendees at Salesforce's Dreamforce conference or the Ford exhibit at the Los Angeles Auto Show or the Coke pavilion at the Olympics engage the exact same content, capture the exact same photos and videos, or post the same messages on social media. One brand engagement can result in millions of different experiences.

CREATING A WIRED EXPERIENCE

The digital live toolkit has expanded over the years. Our studies have uncovered 13 distinct types of Digital Engagement Methods being used in varying degrees across experiential marketing programs.

- *Amplifiers.* Digital elements put in place to amplify the reach of an experience to hundreds, thousands, even millions of people who aren't physically at an event.

Example: The launch of Puma's IGNITE running shoe set off a spectacle in New York City's Times Square that involved semi-professional runners, the NYPD, tourists, and passersby pounding away in their IGNITE footwear on 25 branded treadmills. It was all topped off by an appearance by Puma spokesman and the world's fastest man, Usain Bolt.

Consumers were invited to put on the shoes and try them on a series of running machines. Each machine contained an "energy tracker" that transmitted data to a giant screen placed at the front of the activation. After 150 minutes of running, the screen showcased that the group had reached 100 percent, a feat that prompted an appearance by Bolt, ascending above the crowd on a riser positioned within a semicircular LED tower. This moment was projected on five of Times Square's largest billboards as pyrotechnics flared above the crowds to kick off IGNITE's global launch.

The energy trackers placed on the treadmills were crucial to the activation, serving as the primary measurement tool to gauge the runners' distance. The billboards garnered 125 million impressions with an estimated social media reach of 15.5 million.

- *Feeders.* Using social media and technology as primary drivers of attendance to live experiences and/or to viewership of online streams. Most often requires targets to register for an event on a specific social media channel or platform.

Examples: Smirnoff's Nightlife Exchange Project invited consumers around the world to submit more than 33,000 ideas to facebook.com/smirnoff, and the best of them came to life at 14 events around the globe. Facebook was the only way to register to attend the events (see Chapter 3 for more on this campaign). Elsewhere, Coca-Cola's Summer of Love program in Israel allowed teens to attend a multi-day beach event filled with games, activities, and Coke. The only way to attend was to register on Facebook—and once onsite, attendees were required to sync RFID wristbands to their Facebook accounts so images and content could be auto-posted to the users' social networks.

- *Dialogs.* When target audiences use social media and technology for instant communication with a brand or each other.

Example: HP's Social Everywhere campaign was brought to life with a Social Media Hub and Word Cloud Portraits interactive that generated the best social media metrics ever for HP Discover, its three-day conference.

HP enjoys a sizeable audience through its blogs, LinkedIn, Twitter, and Facebook channels. However, to tap into the potential reach among followers of in-person attendees as well as employees who are active on social media, HP and handling agency Sparks created a comprehensive social media strategy for everyone involved with the show.

The social efforts increased awareness of HP Discover social activity and inspired attendees and employees to participate in the HP Discover social community. The strategy provided at-event social media training and tools to HP employees and stakeholders, such as live tweeting, demo promotion, and influencer development. Attendee Twitter handles, collected during registration, were included on event badges along with HP Discover social accounts. The company promoted the #HPDiscover hashtag on signage throughout the show.

A Social Media Hub, positioned in the lobby just outside of the show floor entrance, literally bridged the digital-physical divide. The Hub displayed HP's Twitter stream, leader boards, and views of real-time social activity such as trending terms and hashtags during the event. Content was displayed on monitors affixed to a curved display wall, positioned to ensure visibility from afar. The Social Media Hub also hosted a Word Cloud Portrait station where attendees could create and share customized images of their faces rendered as word clouds composed of tech-related keywords. The station utilized HP Pro Slate tablets wirelessly linked via a shared application that enabled the portrait creation and sharing in near-real time.

The Word Cloud Portrait application and HP ExploreCloud, which provided the metrics displayed on the large screens, took the social media experience to a whole new level. HP ExploreCloud combined robust data collection, parsing, and analysis capabilities with data visualization to represent, at a glance, the real-time social media activity within specific parameters. It enabled HP to display the social media activity generated by HP accounts and at-show attendees, as well as to showcase the general buzz across the web resulting from the event.

The three-tiered strategy worked together to increase reach and engagement of attendees. More voices joined the conversation, more social accounts were activated, and more content was produced. For the first time ever, the primary event hashtag #HPDiscover trended on two days of the show. And the event saw double-digit growth in overall social media activity during the week of the event, including both HP and non-HP accounts.

- *Extended Views.* Real-time broadcasts of experiential content—usually live video streams, audio feeds, and "back stage"–style exclusive access features—available on a website, social media channel, or mobile app.

Examples: To showcase the versatility of cotton and position cotton as high-end fashion, trade group Cotton Inc. produced a 24-hour live fashion show in Miami's trendy South Beach area, which was streamed live online. Beginning at noon and running until noon the next day, the show featured one fashion "look" per minute for a total of 1,440 outfits that highlighted cotton as a fabric that is fashionable night and day. Each of the 24 hours presented themed categories of cotton apparel, such as "pajama party" and "urban chic."

Elsewhere, Times Square has long been prime real estate for business-to-consumer stunts and activations, but the "Crossroads of the World" has also become a sought-after venue for innovative business-to-business programs. To mark the launch of its two newest motorcycles, Kawasaki busted out of the traditional hotel conference unveil and paired the power of the Big Apple with the reach of the Internet for a memorable product launch targeting its dealers around the country.

The brand executed a three-day takeover of Times Square that was streamed on Kawasaki.com. The live event included stunt shows, appearances by celebrity racers, motorcycle gear fashion shows, and music by DJ Scribble, all as a lead-up to the big reveal of the two new Ninja bikes. A texting contest throughout the day provided the viewing audience with a chance to enter to win one of the two new motorcycles, and 75 dealers supported the event by organizing a ride-in that started in Times Square.

Kawasaki's product launches normally get the message out to 2,500 Kawasaki dealers, but the Times Square event drew over 10,000 people, including dealers, enthusiasts and, as a bonus, consumers. But the live stream was what really revved up the program's reach—the broadcast was viewed more than 1.5 million times.

- *Hashtaggers.* The use of social media hashtags to drive engagement, track dialogs, or measure an experience.

Examples: Heineken set out to give holiday hosts in New York City the chance to upgrade their parties with #SparkMyParty, a "delivery service" for of-age consumers. The social-media-based campaign kicked off in the month of December and invited Heineken fans to tweet to the brand handle using the #SparkMyParty hashtag.

Over the following two days, winners were selected in New York City to receive a party package at their doorsteps. Prizes included JamBox custom playlists, holiday décor, party favors, and a Heineken-branded gift card. In addition to the party pack, four party hosts received an "added spark" in the form of such services as a live DJ, an event photographer to capture their evening's festivities, Uber gift cards for guests, or a roomful of balloons. To extend the campaign further, Heineken opened up #Spark-MyParty beyond New York, selecting consumers from across the country to win their own party packages bearing all the same festive items.

Elsewhere, online retailer Zappos delighted Austin consumers with a unique chase activation that was as weird as the city's self-proclaimed personality. In order to drive traffic and purchases at Zappos.com, the brand sent a life-sized gingerbread man out onto the streets of the city and challenged folks to catch him and take a picture and upload the photos to Twitter with the hashtag #ZapposGingerbreadMan. A street team, outfitted as bakers, chased the escaped Gingerbread Man throughout the city. To build initial buzz, the brand sent packages of custom gingerbread cookies in Zappos boxes to local media outlets and social-savvy companies. Then, on chase day, Zappos encouraged local Austinites, armed with their mobile devices, to join the social hunt based on clues pushed out through the @Zappos Twitter handle. Those consumers who spotted the Gingerbread Man around the city were asked to snap a picture and share his whereabouts. These social actions equated to the capture of the Gingerbread Man, and participants were rewarded with Zappos gift cards. Over the course of the two-day event, 350 Austin consumers earned a reward for capturing the Gingerbread Man, and the social chatter around the event yielded 9.3 million impressions for the brand.

- **Wearables.** A relatively new addition to the experiential marketer's digital toolkit. Uses wearable devices—most often an RFID bracelet but in other cases smartphones and smartwatches—to allow target audiences to trigger experiences and enable brands to measure participants' activity.

Examples: Anyone who has ever been to a giant outdoor music festival knows two things will inevitably happen: You will lose your friends and your phone will die. Fail. Using NFC technology embedded in wristbands, Outside Lands festival sponsor Esurance offered festival-goers a utility to enhance the experience on-site and online, ensuring that they could record memories as well as keep track of their friends. Attendees pre-registered for Insider Band wristbands on a custom branded microsite in the weeks before the festival. They then picked up their wristbands, which were tethered to their Facebook accounts, at the Esurance booth on-site. At any of eight 14-foot tap towers located throughout the grounds, festival-goers could tap the band to take a photo. Photos could be immediately uploaded or saved to a "Digital Memory Bank" to access and share from a microsite after the event. Festival-goers could also tap a tower to find out whether they'd instantly won a cool prize, like ticket upgrades; or tap to save content such as set lists or drinks they liked at Outside Lands' famous Beer and Wine Lands. Most conveniently, attendees could tap towers to check in at different stages, see where their friends had checked in, and leave messages. Each tower featured branding, a call to action, and a screen above the "tap" button.

Alternatively, the towers enabled Esurance to increase its visibility on-site. In fact, the brand ended up being the only overarching brand at Wine and Beer Lands. The towers were frequently used as meeting points for non-Insider Band users, too. So, regardless of participation in the program, the brand made an impression with every festival-goer. Ultimately, Esurance was able to drive home a key marketing message: that through its commitment to technology, it can help change how consumers purchase and manage insurance for the better. The effort also helped launch Esurance into the hot wearable tech conversation, generating buzz for Esurance in the tech community well beyond the festival. The brand received press from Mashable twice, and from the *San Francisco Chronicle*, among other major news outlets.

The NFC-wristband program recorded some nine "taps" per wearer, or 18 taps per minute and 10,000 taps total per day, resulting in 1,857,000-plus social media impressions. On top of that, 66 percent of participants re-engaged with Esurance by visiting the "Digital Memory Bank" after the event—an unprecedented percentage compared to typical sponsorship opportunities that do not extend beyond the event.

Elsewhere, Miller Genuine Draft went to Panama to bring a taste of its brand to ValleBash, the electronic dance music festival held every year in the mountains for an exclusive, invite-only crew of Facebook influencers. For the brand, this was the ideal environment to leverage its EDM associations, while grabbing an opportunity to be associated with an influential group of consumers on their terms, in their world.

MGD tapped into a variety of technologies to make its impression, including 3-D projections fed onto screens designed to replicate Panama City's skyline. The brand hosted live vj performances and pushed social media amplification via branded RFID wristbands and readers that captured partygoers enjoying time with friends and the MGD, which was the exclusive beer on site. Once authorized, photos of the bash were posted on Facebook. The projections punched up the crowd, but the integration of RFID technology into the ValleBash live experience increased delivery of product messaging for the brand and permitted MGD to track ROI against sponsorship investment and capture valuable consumer data post-event to help determine additional exposure generated. By the end of the festival, 60 percent of the attendees authorized Facebook posts (pretty good for a group considered to be among the savviest of Facebook influencers), and each attendee made about 2.2 total social posts from the event.

Elsewhere, for Microsoft's Worldwide Partner Conference, RFID wristbands served as the centerpiece of an event-wide strategy that was designed to facilitate networking, enhance the on-site experience, and fuel collaboration among Microsoft's U.S. partner ecosystem (see Chapter 4 for more on this program). The bands also acted as a real-world and real-time showpiece for Microsoft's technologies, giving attendees a contextual experience with how the company's products work and integrate with one another. For example, activations at every location (which included the Ritz Hotel, Orlando Conference Center, and Disney

Epcot) were linked together via the Microsoft Azure cloud. Microsoft Surface tablets with QR code and RFID scanners were used to register attendees.

The attendee experience began upon arrival at the Microsoft U.S. Regional Lounge, where partners registered and connected their RFID bands with their Facebook, Twitter, and e-mail credentials. Attendees were able to scan QR codes from their mobile phones to easily transfer their registration information to the LED-enabled wristbands.

Over the course of the week, the bands fueled multiple types of attendee engagements and streamlined information gathering into a paper-free experience. Strategically located tap stands and scan-to-share stands at all of the events enabled Microsoft to deliver key event information such as calendar updates and event details, encouraged social sharing of the onsite activities including photos, and connected guests to information delivered to their inboxes. A sharing feature provided Microsoft with a permission-based opt-in that could amplify branded content on guests' personal social pages.

Attendees could also use their wristbands to gain entry to exclusive functions, including an Epcot after-hours event where the event technology actually *replaced* Disney's in-house MagicBand and photo systems on the final evening of the conference, and granted attendees the ability to participate in the park's finale fireworks show. The LED components of attendees' wristbands could be controlled by a special infrared network set up throughout Epcot that lit up the bands as attendees entered special zones where customized activations such as photo kiosks were stationed.

Although they were small, the bands were mighty, delivering a constant stream of data points that the company could track in real time, including registration participation by social network, traffic at each activation area across geography, number of photos, check-ins, information shares, and more. In the end, the RFID bands were used by more than 6,000 attendees, generated more than 4,000 check-ins and photos, and overall contributed to 8,000 engagements with WPC-related content for a total reach of 4.2 million.

And as marketers become more comfortable with technology and social media, they begin to accelerate their use of multiple types and formats. For the 2015 International Fight Week, the Ultimate Fighting

Championship (UFC) wanted to take the potential for amplification to the next level and deliver unprecedented access to fans. The resulting event technology strategy was just as unprecedented as the objective, with the brand live-wiring the entire host city of Las Vegas. Tens of thousands of fans could simply tap their UFC credentials (via RFID/ NFC badge, wristband, or QR code) throughout the city to earn UFC Rewards points, snap photos, participate in leader boards, and gain exclusive access to pool and viewing parties—and then instantly share their experiences on social networks. The campaign, dubbed Las Vegas TakeOver, also included the integration of sponsor activations by Reebok, Kraft, Bud Light, Monster Energy, Toyo Tires, Harley-Davidson, EA Sports, MusclePharm, UFC Gym, and MetroPCS.

Tap stations dotted the city from pools to hotel lobby kiosks, to the route of a 5K run and along the Las Vegas Monorail, and spanned not only from one end of the Strip to the other, but also Fremont Street, Red Rock Resort, and Hendersonville. A UFC Mobile app tied all the elements together, keeping fans aware of all the activities and delivering unique content. The campaign unleashed hundreds of devices: laptops, tablets, handhelds, rewards check-in kiosks, drones for video, RFID readers, QR scanners, touch screens, DSLR cameras, mobile devices, video cameras, and the Microsoft Azure Cloud infrastructure that linked all the devices together.

Among the knockout results from UFC TakeOver was increased throughput. Wait times to meet fighters went from hours in 2014 to minutes in 2015, thanks to the wearables integration. UFC fan amplification also resulted in millions of friends interacting with branded content that was curated at venues throughout Las Vegas during the week. More than 13,000 fans participated in at least one activation, with many fans participating in as many as 85 activations.

- *Virtual Reality.* Using VR technology within experiential engagements is gaining popularity as availability of technology increases and decreasing pricing puts the technology within reach of marketers' budgets. Oculus Rift headsets are the most prevalent hardware being used for creating VR experiences.

Example: Outdoor shoe brand Merrell has enjoyed a long history of loyalty among serious hikers and outdoor enthusiasts. But it was in need of a little extra adrenaline to shed its "brown shoe" reputation and get younger audiences excited about its brand. Enter the Sundance Film Festival, one of the world's only events where lovers of the great outdoors rub elbows with lovers of art, film, and pop culture for a week every January. Merrell jumped into the festival scene with "TrailScape," a hair-raising Oculus Rift experience that transported consumers to the rocky Dolomites in the Italian Alps for a mountain hike that showcased the brand's newest and most advanced hiking shoe, the Capra, named after the Capra mountain goat.

Attendees needed all their wits and balance to brave treacherous virtual rock ledges and swinging bridges. Oscar-winning effects house, Framestore, added 4-D elements such as rumbling floors to simulate a rockslide and gusts of wind at the peak, to help immerse guests in the experience. But the real showstopper was the introduction of an obstacle course—an element made possible by a first-of-its-kind spatial-mapping software technology that, unlike most stationary Oculus Rift experiences, allowed participants to move freely through a virtual environment by also *actually walking* through a physical space.

Guests stepped into a padded obstacle course and put on the Oculus Rift headset. They were then transported to a mountain pathway mirroring the layout of the physical environment. As they moved about, participants pressed themselves against walls and inched along a narrow mountain ledge, and screamed as they jumped back when ledges in front of them crumbled, sending rocky debris down a sheer mountain face. Real-world rope railings were firmly grasped as users navigated a precarious suspension bridge in the VR world.

- *Content Generation.* Integrating social media and technology into live experiences for the expressed purpose of stimulating user-generated content capture and sharing. In some cases, audiences decide what to share and when. In other cases, content is captured and automatically posted on their social media channels.

Example: Whether they were supporting Barack Obama or Mitt Romney, coffee drinkers around the country got to cast their votes in the 7-Eleven Mobile Oval. The cross-country tour was devoted to sampling 7-Eleven coffee, but its hook was challenging consumers to see whether they could predict the outcome of the 2012 presidential election.

Participants voted by choosing either a blue (Obama) or red (Romney) cup. To deepen the engagement, guests were escorted through a "metal detector" and scrutinized by a "secret service agent," before being invited to enjoy a cup of coffee at a replica of the president's desk in the Oval Office. A "press aide" greeted guests and piloted them to a seat behind the desk, which was complete with a red phone.

Guests received a commemorative photo that was digitally framed, branded, automatically uploaded to their social networks, and sent to their e-mail for further sharing. The photos also were immediately uploaded to the 7-Eleven Facebook page. Each participant also received a commemorative coffee tumbler that he or she could refill numerous times for 99 cents at 7-Eleven.

By voting with their coffee cups, Mobile Oval guests accurately projected the outcome of the election, as 7-Eleven doled out more blue cups than red ones. The tour garnered considerable press online and in print, and the brand hit its goals for sampling and social media.

Elsewhere, Hyundai's Re:Mix Lab featured a series of events targeting Millennials with content-driven experiences that included tricked-out cars, cutting-edge speakers, and an artifact retrospective called Exhibits in Collaboration. Each event showcased three vehicles that had been modified to represent a lifestyle theme. The Music 2.0 Veloster Turbo, for example, featured a chrome exterior and a motorized touch-screen DJ station on a large-screen TV that allowed consumers to spin tunes from the trunk.

Attendees enjoyed cocktails and hors d'oeuvres, live music, keynote lectures, and DJ sets, all carefully curated to appeal to the local market and the Millennial sharing mindset. Fourteen museum-quality displays composed Exhibits in Collaboration, a series of static exhibits that showcased one-of-a-kind artifacts from collaborations in art, music, and design, such as bottles from the collaboration between French DJ David Guetta and Coca-Cola. Guests could instantly share their experiences on Facebook through interactive RFID bracelets scanned at kiosks.

By the end of the seven-city tour, 48,850 attendees had shared content about their Re:Mix experiences with more than 23 million of their friends.

Another Content Generation example is the first-ever reality show created by a brand, driven by consumers, and broadcast on network TV. Ford's "Escape Routes" was a six-part televised series of "Amazing Race"–style challenges in which six pairs of best friends vied for a Ford Escape and $100,000. Consumers supported their favorite contestants in their challenges online via live chats, streams, and social media shares, and NBC carried the one-hour show in prime time on Saturday nights while supporting the program across its broadcast, mobile, print, and digital channels. The unusual twist on media partnerships earned Ford its most successful pre-launch campaign to date.

In the months before the campaign, Ford recruited six teams from contestants who submitted videos, ultimately selecting finalists based on the reach of their social networks. Each team was given a Ford Escape and instructed to build an online following that could help them in their weekly challenges.

Virtual teammates could win prizes of their own, too, for chatting, tweeting, recruiting, commenting, playing online games, and participating in interactive challenges. At a challenge in Miami, for example, each team had to livestream with fans to help unlock their cell phones. The teams urged their followers to visit a URL that had been set on their phones and then work together to beat the game and reveal the phone's passcode. Once unlocked, the teams received a text message to take a snapshot of their best "fish face" and then get their followers to re-tweet it 150 times. When that was done, the teams participated in a physical challenge (it was livestreamed, too) that highlighted a feature of the Ford Escape. Live Twitter wrap-ups moderated by a digital host and engagements with bloggers in each market helped the brand beef up its presence online.

By the time the last challenge had been accepted, the interactive TV show had earned Ford 7.7 million viewers. During the program, Escape boosted its share of voice among small SUVs with 116 million tweets, 64 million Facebook impressions, more than 65,000 Facebook "likes" and 3.4 million incremental user-generated video views.

- *Crowdsourced Interactives.* Leveraging technology and social media in ways that allow target audiences to control or customize their experiences.

Examples: The Super Bowl is a perennially cluttered environment, with major brands vying for share of mind among fans onsite and at home. For Super Bowl XLIX in Phoenix, Verizon re-activated and reinvented a successful strategy deployed for the previous year's Super Bowl with a social media campaign that measured fan votes through a custom algorithm and converted them into a spectacular lightshow in downtown Phoenix. It was all fueled by the same hashtag and call to action: #WhosGonnaWin.

All tweets, Instagram posts, and comments on Facebook with the hashtag and reference to one of the Super Bowl teams were captured as a vote. The votes were counted and compared daily to reveal the team that had the most support, revealing "WhosGonnaWin" through a dramatic lightshow. The tabulation of the votes could be refreshed daily to show how the game was heating up and how support was shifting between teams. Additionally, the votes could be broken down by time and location, leading to a series of engaging visual representations of data.

For four consecutive nights, two sides of the Bank of America building came to life in the lead-up to the Super Bowl with a projection mapping show. Fans gathered at the base of the building, and soon these "watch parties" became a hot spot of increased dwell time and stronger brand attribution for Verizon. The show was also livestreamed on WhosGonnaWin.com and NFL Mobile, exclusively from Verizon.

In order to track the voting, the team developed a unique social media algorithm that tracked fan voting across Facebook, Twitter, and Instagram. The algorithm tracked use of the campaign hashtag, combined with the fan sentiment, to determine which users were voting for what teams. In addition, the conversation was tracked geographically so that fans could see where votes for their favorite team were coming from in real time.

Verizon leveraged sports talent to generate buzz for the campaign, drive media attention, and draw fans to the watch parties. A number of current and former players were enlisted from either existing endorsement deals or one-off deals for the Super Bowl in order to amplify the social media campaign even further and share the brand story.

It's not every day that fans are able to see their social engagement impact a larger-than-life experience, and ultimately, the campaign helped position Verizon as a technology leader. All told, there were 576,000 total votes on social, 50 percent mentioning Verizon. Also, there were over one million hits on WhosGonnaWin.com, 169.2 million earned impressions, and 15,000 total viewers on the ground.

- *Hyper Participatory.* The second leading use of social media and technology in experiences, integrating digital layers to drive longer, deeper, and more resonating interactives between a brand and a target audience.

Example: When American Express celebrated its twentieth anniversary as a sponsor of the U.S. Open Tennis Championship, the brand set out to establish itself in consumers' minds as a technology player with the Art and Sound of Tennis inside an on-site American Express Fan Experience.

The strategy connected with attendees' passion for the sport by giving them a personalized and deeply participatory opportunity to make something beautiful and shareable. The brand invited cardholders and non-cardholders to pick up a tennis racket, step into a tennis bay, and show off their swings. Every forehand and backhand was digitally translated into a work of art. The company supplied guests with rackets that had embedded chips to measure the speed, direction, and velocity of each person's swing. A custom bit of software took the information from the sensors and analyzed it. Those results became brush strokes that combined to create an illustration, shown on the LED screen in the activation area.

It wasn't all about the visuals, either. Audio was played and also responded to the swings, increasing volume for faster swings. Every two to three minutes, a new consumer stepped inside to give it a try. When they were done, the brand digitally captured all participants' works of art and e-mailed it to them to share with their friends and family on their personal social platforms. More than 14,000 Tennis Open attendees visited the American Express experience and participated in the Art

& Sound of Tennis activation. They weren't afraid to share their creations, either. In fact, Amex showed a 600 percent increase in social media engagement over the previous year.

- *Geo-gagements.* Uses location detection—usually via a mobile app or BLE beacons—to manage an experience and serve up relevant messages and communication.

Example: New Balance opened its first North American Experience store in the Flatiron district of New York City, and to get the buzz building and shoppers through the doors, for four weeks the brand challenged runners throughout the five boroughs to "race for the chance to win" free shoes, gift cards, and, for one grand prize winner, a solid gold New Balance Baton worth $20,000.

The program invited local runners to download an app called Urban Dash. The app used phone GPS functionality to show the runners' positions in relation to virtual "batons" dropped all over the city. To pick up the baton, a runner had to get within 100 feet of it to virtually pick it up, then run to the New Balance store before another runner stole it. For a steal, players could get within 100 feet of another player, allowing one runner's app to swipe the baton from another. Once a runner arrived at the store, brand ambassadors rewarded him or her with prizes and encouragement to continue picking up additional batons.

- *Social Currency.* The act of exchanging access to an experience, a special offer, or exclusive content for a social media mention or post. (Also see the overview of Currency in Chapter 3.)

Example: Hyundai wanted a way to engage thousands of NCAA fans with football on their minds without being intrusive. To do that, the brand positioned itself as the coolest tailgater in the fan zone with its Show Your Loyalty College Football campaign. The Hyundai FieldHouse installation accomplished its objective with room to spare at each game played by the 25 teams sponsored by Hyundai.

Fans entered the space for a snack and a seat while they watched the ESPN pre-game show. They stayed to take photos with their friends and left with a vintage-inspired university T-shirt. The space was full of football-themed games, Hyundai vehicles with home team branding from each school, and co-branded giveaways. In order to extend beyond the on-site activations, every FieldHouse activity fed social media through RFID integration.

Whenever visitors swiped their RFID key chains, they earned a chance to win an all-new Hyundai Veloster. In addition, every swipe sent a FieldHouse-themed update to Facebook, reaching an average of 160 Facebook friends per swipe, and adding up to more than 1.7 million Facebook impressions. More than 23,000 guests checked into the Field-House throughout the season. Inside local dealerships in each targeted market, the brand also deployed "Love Your Team. Love Your Car" showroom kits that included team-branded signage, mugs, padfolios, and showroom media.

- *Viral Lifters.* Experiences created with the specific purpose of recording them and posting the content on social media platforms, usually YouTube.

Example: OfficeMax during the holiday season unleashed 400 elves across New York City's Union Square to hype the return of its popular ElfYourself website, where consumers can upload headshots of themselves onto the humorously gyrating bodies of dancing elves. Before the brand could upload the street campaign footage to the web, onlookers and passersby had already done so via their phones and cameras. OfficeMax's viral video generated more than 350,000 views on YouTube alone and generated more than 110 million impressions.

CONNECTING ONLINE AND OFF

The combination of digital and live engagements continues to be refined as marketers calibrate the perfect mix of mass-reach online engagement and intimate one-on-one experiences. No matter what the brand or category, CMOs are unanimous when they agree that experiential campaigns that fuse the two realms are at the heart of future marketing successes.

Chapter Six   Experience Design

The growth of experiential marketing spawned a global creative Renaissance and, as a result, a new design discipline formed: experience design.

Experience design represents the consolidation of a dozen design silos (including architecture, industrial design, theatrical design, and graphic design) into a single creative platform. The first mainstream multi-disciplinary creative format, experience design is critical to the success of experiential marketing in that it provides both form and function—and dictates the look and feel of live experiences. Experience design fuses strategy, creativity, and structure to communicate a message to a defined audience and stimulate a specific and pre-determined reaction.

Experiential *marketing* drives a brand's strategy, but experience *design* translates that strategy into living, breathing, shareable moments. Only when you combine the strategy of experiential marketing with the engagement of experience design can you allow people to *feel* your brand.

Upwards of 90 percent of information transmitted to the brain is visual. And because we absorb images 50 times faster than we absorb words, a brand experience is the fastest way to impact the hearts and minds of an audience—and motivate action. Experience design succeeds when it encourages and creates connections, both among the participants within a space and between those participants and a designed environment.

CREATING LIVING STORIES

The best experiences are designed around, and based upon, a story. "Stories are the vehicles that we use to condense and remember experiences, and to communicate them in a variety of situations to certain audiences," notes artificial intelligence theorist and cognitive psychologist Roger Schank. Philosopher John Dewey's theories of expression and creativity define experiences as "moments in time that have a beginning and an end—and change the target audience."

Experience design is heavily influenced by theatrical design in that most live experiences are based on a narrative, using design to create a space that supports a story. Writing a narrative for Oracle's Open-World event, for example, is not unlike scripting a multi-act theatrical play. The essential rules of theatrical engagements apply to marketing experiences:

- Rule 1. Space is not static.
- Rule 2. Transitions are important.
- Rule 3. A grand entrance has impact.
- Rule 4. Lighting and sound enhance the experience.
- Rule 5. Great experiences are designed around great journeys through space.

As mentioned in Chapter 1, live experiences use the ancient building blocks of engagement-based narrative (exposition, conflict, catharsis, resolution) to explain, educate, engage, and inform audiences. No matter what the brand, product, or service, these experience building blocks never change—it's how marketers arrange them and build on them that does. There are seven elements that comprise experiential story structure:

- *The Premise*. The underlying theme. The point or goal of the story. In experience design, this is the objective/goal of the event/experience.

- *Characters.* Common people/places/things that show up and develop throughout the story. In experience design, characters can be brands, products, attendees, even technology.
- *Crucible.* Gives reason to the "space" the story takes place in. Why this space? Why this amount of time in that space? In live experiences, the best stories have a connection to the space in which they play out—and the spaces are selected because they support the Premise.
- *Protagonist.* Traditionally labeled as "the good" of the story. In live experiences, this is the hero brand or product.
- *Antagonist.* Traditionally labeled as "the bad" of the story or the protagonist's barrier. In experiences, this is the problem or challenge that the Premise and Characters are designed to change or overcome.
- *Arches.* The character chapters, the changes of a plot—the progression of the story. Live experiences are designed using story arches, allowing audiences to engage, initiate, and absorb the experience over time.
- *Conflict.* The tension of the story; the "reason" the characters are trying to succeed. Put in perspective for live events, this is an issue that will be resolved or some friction that will be eased.

Once the story building blocks are mapped, it must be translated into the Touchpoint Blueprint (Figure 6.1), which uses five pillars to further develop the brand experience:

- *Engagement Backstory.* Leverage past history, past experiences, and changing audience dynamics to understand how this audience has been engaged before. You will use that history to develop the content and engagement strategy for future experiences.
- *Setting.* Determine the space you will use and how it will be created or leveraged to connect with audiences and tell the story.
- *Branded Characters.* Consider how the brand will be positioned and used across the experience—the qualities or emotions the brand will exhibit and elicit across the people, places, and things put into the space.

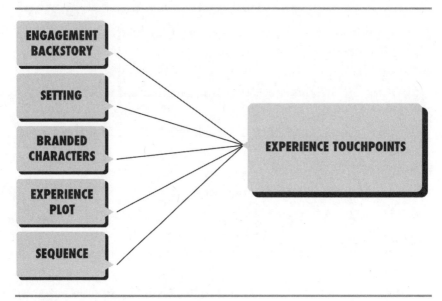

FIGURE 6.1   Touchpoint Blueprint

- *Experience Plot.* Program what will happen. How will your audience and your brand come together? We also refer to this as the "Experience Agenda" or "Live Flow."
- *Sequence.* Design the specific touchpoints that will connect the experience to the audience.

BUILDING AN EXPERIENCE

With the story and touchpoints assembled, it's time to design an experience that touches all of our Experience Design Quadrants: Product/Service, Environment, Communication, and Behavior (Figure 6.2). Around these four quadrants are three "outer engagement rings"—Brand Values, Product Benefits, and Brand Impact. If the experience delivers on all four quadrants and is supported by all outer rings, the design is considered to be "calibrated" and ready for full development.

Next, compare and contrast the brand's wants with the audience's needs. The best experience designs are based on these intersections. An example of such a design is the exhibit that TurboChef created to launch

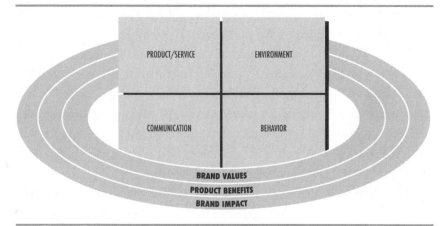

FIGURE 6.2   Experience Design Quadrants

a new speed-cook oven at the Kitchen and Bath Industry Show. The company wanted to communicate the professional performance of its ovens in a home environment, but had to overcome concerns with how the units looked in a home kitchen and what speed-cooked food tastes like. The common ground was the product and the food that comes out of it, so the company designed an environment that focused first on this and second on architecture. The focal point of the experience was a restaurant-style cooking bar with soft, rounded edges and warm wood surfaces that connected the product to the home kitchen. More importantly, performance and taste questions were answered through cooking presentations during which celebrity chef Charlie Trotter demonstrated the Turbo Chef in action.

The physical look and feel of an experience connects with participants' minds, and moves their bodies through the space. Correct and calibrated experiences are designed around six tenets:

Tenet 1. Start Early

Smart marketers trigger emotions in advance by creating initiatives that start long before the target arrives at the venue, street corner, or retail space. Long before Katy Perry rode into the Super Bowl Halftime Show on a larger-than-life tiger puppet, Pepsi was making sure fans could hear its sponsorship roar. To drive unprecedented excitement for one of the most highly anticipated events of the year, and seamlessly tie its brand to it, Pepsi and agency Motive brought the Hyped for Halftime campaign it launched in 2013 back for a return engagement in 2014—once again, the proprietary platform allowed Pepsi to bring the magic of halftime to unexpected places and times across America. Pepsi's Super Bowl program offered a supreme lesson in scaling an experience, with touchpoints that ranged from live events to digital content and visibility in Super Bowl host city Phoenix. While the halftime show runs a little under 15 minutes, Pepsi's experiences lasted days, and beyond, across all its channels.

The launch began on Thanksgiving with a massive concert experience featuring multiplatinum country artist Blake Shelton. He performed for more than 3,000 military veterans on the deck of the *USS Lexington* in Corpus Christi, Texas. The event was captured by renowned director Samuel Bayer and transformed into both a 60-second TV commercial airing during the biggest game of the holiday lineup, as well as a two-minute digital content piece to help kick off a string of Hyped for Halftime experiences leading up to the big game.

Among larger consumer-driven moments was the national Hype Your Hometown program that encouraged thousands of fans to upload photos and videos to showcase their own over-the-top hype for a chance to bring a once-in-a-lifetime halftime show to their neck of the woods. In the end, Rochester, New York, took home the prize, playing host to singers Nico & Vinz on a giant outdoor stage downtown with more than 7,500 in attendance. Once in Phoenix for the big game, Pepsi made its presence known with a series of outdoor advertisements spanning higher than 30 stories, along with an on-street engagement experience that helped fans reach "maximum" levels of hype right up until kickoff on Super Bowl Sunday. Pepsi amassed a total of more than 3.7 billion impressions, including 126 million media impressions and 38 content pieces with a combined 116 million views on the web. On the ground, Pepsi events attracted more than 10,000 attendees over three days of concerts and other surprises.

Tenet 2. Drive Trial

Look deep into the best live experiences, and you'll find elements that not only build a brand but are closely tied to its business as well. Through thousands of one-on-one interactions with its target audience, Google focused on how Chromebooks can be incorporated into the everyday routines of college students, bringing the value proposition to life in a way that was relevant and personal. Allowing individuals to test-drive a technology product for an extended period offered a unique experience seldom employed by other tech brands.

For students at a dozen college campuses across the country, taking a trip to the library went from stale to stimulating as Google's lending experience took hold. The technology titan's six-week national tour put its lightweight and speedy Chromebook laptops directly into the hands of college students who were invited to borrow the devices from sleek pop-up libraries positioned in highly visible locations at the heart of campus life.

Leveraging the insight that students increasingly work in the cloud and often lug their heavy laptops with them to class, Google's activation was designed to allow students to take Chromebooks for a multi-day test-drive and experience its benefits first-hand. Playing off the classic library metaphor, Google temporarily hunkered down at public and private universities across the United States, where students could get personalized demos and check out a Chromebook for up to four days. To borrow and return devices, the Lending Library was open four days a week from 10 a.m. to 4 p.m., which was identified as the most popular time to be on campus.

Google and agency Grow Marketing placed high-top tables directly in front of the Lending Library, offering a place for students to set up their Chromebooks, connect to free Wi-Fi, and chat with friends or finish homework between classes. Perhaps the most buzz-worthy element of the activation, however, was the "surprise pop" component. Taking a cue from the Willy Wonka golden ticket experience, Google placed surprise tickets into 30 random Chromebooks at select campuses. During the checkout process, a member of the lending crew opened the laptop and, if it included a ticket, handed the lucky student a brand new Chromebook to keep.

Post-event surveys indicated a high purchase consideration rate among students who engaged in the activation. In addition, the pop-up experience generated 1.54 million #ChromebookforCollege hashtag impressions on Twitter.

Tenet 3. Use the Space

A venue is a canvas—it's not "the" experience. And the best spaces are not always the right spaces. We've seen events held at the most gorgeous venues in the most exotic cities fall flat—and events held inside empty warehouses or on street corners win awards. "Spaces have lives as you move through them," designer David Rockwell told us in 2010.

But space *does* dictate the type of experience that can be created. In some cases, companies have total control over a space. These are "controlled experiences"; brands have the power to transform the space as much or as little as the narrative dictates. In other cases, companies must create an experience they can control inside one they cannot. These are "chaos experiences," where companies design and control a certain portion or piece of the space. Trade shows are examples of chaos experiences—groups of companies, hundreds or even thousands of them, massed together within a single space delivering completely different experiences.

Over the last few years, we've seen both types of experiences evolve. Controlled experiences use total space takeovers to create completely branded immersions. Google's annual I/O event in San Francisco, for example, presented a strategic and forward-thinking design to the developer community in 2014—an aesthetic built on a carefully crafted theme using light, surface, and movement to create a consistent look and a more enjoyable experience for attendees. The subdued design offered a warm and hip aesthetic, a departure from the brand's scrappy, playful past. Whenever possible, it incorporated Bay-area touches, such as local street artists who created large-scale digital prints for the massive fabric walls covering the brick façade inside the building.

On the outside of Moscone Center, unmistakable 30-foot I/O branding used a 20-foot Google Map pin marking the spot for event goers. A full redesign of the event in conjunction with agency Sparks incorporated warmer tones and materials. Exposed plywood edges created a sophisticated industrial approach for registration and welcome structures, partner demo areas, and interactive displays. Custom furniture, including a "lounge mountain," offered spaces for attendees to chat, climb, and code.

A sandbox area on the second level hosted 12 partner pods, rather than the 100 of years past. Sixteen-foot signage towers identified areas of interest, and A-frames were used for way-finding in lieu of traditional meter board signs. Two cloud-like forms hovering above the area served as a massive visual focal point. Adjacent to the sandbox, a 6,000-square-foot Code Lab focused on the needs of developers and web designers. Numerous pop-up spaces featured additional speakers and white boards with monitors where people could interact in less formal areas. The third level presented Google products and services in lifestyle vignettes, including Build with Chrome, which featured a digital LEGO activity.

Meanwhile, designers of chaos experiences have found success with two different strategies. Some have embraced "amplified simplicity," using clean architecture and an intentionally simplified experience flow to their advantage, essentially using less chaos to make noise inside existing chaos. Others use "contrast" to their advantage, with an experience that goes against the grain to do something different from what others in the space are doing—instead of creating a traditional single 80-by-80 exhibit, some may instead use 10 or 20 inline booths in a row—using that stark contrast as a magnet. In these cases, companies look at the overall event as the static or dynamic and then create a reverse—a contrast. Sometimes it's the space that inspires the concept. (A friend once illustrated these static-dynamic relationships this way: If you take a pink sofa from the lobby of a Ritz-Carlton and place it in a large field of grass, the color changes through the experience and space that is used.)

Attendees at chaos-laden Comic-Con got to participate in an obstacle course that replicated the look and feel of 18th century Paris and learn how to move like an assassin, achieving the same stunts in real life that they perform virtually in Ubisoft's Assassin's Creed Unity game. They rolled, vaulted, and raced their way across the course, which included large set pieces, cannons, and custom propaganda flyers, performing moves inspired by military obstacle course training (called "parkour"), sprinting across rooftops, dodging cannon balls, and diving off a 25-foot Leap of Faith. Participants could also play the game on custom gaming kiosks, which stimulated on-site pre-orders of the game. Those who completed the course earned an Assassin's Creed Experience T-shirt. The course was specially designed by Ubisoft's chief parkour officer and Tempest Freerunning Academy, the world's top freerunners, assuring it would be a professional parkour-grade experience.

Throughout the day, the course played host to professional parkour athletes from Tempest dressed in period attire. These athletes put on a show, illustrating the storyline of the game, and captivating attendees. These shows were filmed, creating compelling content for digital amplification and engaging thousands of fans in the experience. But perhaps the most impressive aspect of the experience was the enormous footprint that pushed the boundaries of temporary event construction.

Tenet 4. Put Time on Your Side

The best way to form a relationship with customers is to create a longer engagement with them. We remember the CMO of a global liquor company telling us that market research showed that, when brand ambassadors explained one of his spirits brands to consumers in under a minute, less than 3 percent ever ordered his whiskey. But when brand ambassadors discussed the brand for more than three minutes, 10 percent of consumers ordered. His next move? Mandating that no dialog with the consumer be less than three minutes.

For marketers trained in an advertising economy, success has long been measured in 30-second increments multiplied by frequency. As we've already discussed, it's a model that can only pay back reach, never real engagement. But the traditional media model did teach marketers to put a value on time. Experience design gives companies the ability to actually design an engagement around a specific length of time. Put another way, if you know how long a conversation you need with your target, you can actually design an experience based on what we call the Necessary Experience Dialog (NED).

Translation: Marketers are now using experiences as a time machine—and the best brands create them, extend them, and measure them. Time is the ultimate experiential ROI multiplier. Every second you can spend with an audience has a value. When we look at behavioral and learning modalities, emotion, and attention, they all factor into the totality of an experience—and the actual amount of time a brand connects with customers powers it all. The extension of time multiplies efficacy. Increased time increases the opportunity to create a relationship—and more relationships extend to the bottom line.

Tenet 5. A Balanced Experience

Too often we find the essence of a brand is assumed by a company. But many marketers don't know their brands as well as they think. Why? Because most brands have never been unleashed into a live setting. Most marketers assume they know how consumers interact with their brands—but watching it happen in front of your eyes is very different and is usually an eye-opening exercise. Our point? That in order to design an experience, marketers need to begin with a relevant portrait of their brand and use it as the anchor of the design process.

Ensuring the live experience brings to life that essence, or DNA, of the brand requires a seven-step experience discovery process:

- *Step 1. The X-ray (Situational Analysis).* Marketers analyze the brand itself—what it means, what it stands for, what elements help it connect with the target audience. Often this is also a discovery of the target audience in tandem with brand objectives. Sometimes it's also a gap analysis, uncovering the difference between what the company thinks its brand means and what it actually does connote.
- *Step 2. Diagrammatic Development (Defining the Opportunity and Scope).* This step extracts the knowledge from the X-ray and constructs an effective solution against the objectives.
- *Step 3. Ideation Genesis (Creative Solution).* Initial ideas and scope of the experience are developed based on Steps 1 and 2.
- *Step 4. Validation and Vetting (Market and Audience Testing and Confirmation).* Using data, historical results, and audience insights, ideas are vetted and eventually validated.
- *Step 5. Design Development (Final Program Construction).* Full experience design solution and program are approved and moved into development stage.
- *Step 6. Activation Commencement (Program Roll-Out).* The actual construction and execution of the live experience solution.
- *Step 7. Evaluation (Measurement).* Analysis of the program across predetermined data fields and objectives. It's important to note that beginning with an analytical exercise in Step 1 creates the glue for the eventual solution. The process ensures marketers aren't making arbitrary design decisions but rather balancing the wants and needs of the target audience against the brand's primary objective.

Tenet 6. Connect Digital and Live

Technology has become as prominent a tool in the experience designer's toolkit as traditional architecture and graphics. The days of structure-heavy experiences have been replaced by an era of digitally integrated engagements in which media and architecture combine. This new frontier represents significant opportunities for designers who for too long anchored their experiences in mere physical architecture. Digital design has collided with the world of architecture and changed how companies think about and activate their experiential strategies.

Put another way, brands are flipping the media-and-architecture model on its head, creating full media experiences and then translating them into physical spaces. *Example:* To celebrate its twentieth birthday, Old Navy wanted to blow out the candles in style. And, like any modern 20-year-old, the brand wanted the party to be big, bold, and full of shareable moments. The answer? A #selfiebration. Promoting its fundamental brand tenets of fun, family, and fashion, Old Navy created a digital and physical birthday party, which allowed consumers to connect with the brand in a memorable and inclusive way.

The #selfiebration featured a one-of-kind 42-foot-tall balloon billboard composed of 960 balloons that were 16 times thicker than traditional balloons. The balloons expanded in real time to form personalized "balloon selfies" for each participating consumer. Participants engaged with brand ambassadors to join the #selfiebration in New York City's Times Square and at L.A.'s Hollywood and Highland. Participants watched their selfies "blow up" and subsequently shared their experiences via their personal social media channels, generating organic chatter and creating content for the brand. Those who couldn't attend the bash in person joined the digital party. Using Twitter, users uploaded their selfies along with their ultimate birthday wishes to @OldNavy using the hashtag #selfiebration.

In response, users received a unique party favor—a digitally rendered image of their balloon close-ups—and a chance to have their wildest birthday wishes come true. Each participant on Twitter also received an exclusive coupon code for in-store and online purchases. Digitally, #selfiebration was the most successful program in Old Navy's 20-year history. The campaign generated 17,498 uses of the #selfiebration hashtag, 640 million media impressions, and 13,669 contest entries, while increasing social media engagement by 414 percent.

Elsewhere, online car insurance company Esurance promises customers an "intuitive, hassle-free insurance experience." It used an official sponsorship of the South by Southwest (SXSW) event in Austin to identify two shared equities between its brand and SXSW that would help connect with attendees. One: Time is precious. SXSW attendees want to see as much as possible in a very short window. Esurance is all about freeing up time to do the things you love. And two: Unpreparedness is a pain point. SXSW is big, especially for newcomers, so if you don't know what to seek out, it can be overwhelming. Similarly, the world of insurance is complex and can be equally overwhelming. The resulting strategy focused on simplifying the SXSW experience through technology to enable attendees to get the most out of their time—and to cultivate a little brand love for Esurance in the process.

The activation played out in two phases. In part one, called the Dream Gig, a pre-event Facebook promotion sent one Esurance fan to SXSW as a brand correspondent. While there, the winner helped produce daily branded recap videos. Esurance leveraged Facebook's Open Graph SDK to create a fully integrated social content submission platform that drove the entry and amplification process for all entries. This allowed individuals to quickly and easily share their entries to garner votes via their social communities. The strategy also brought the Esurance message to a wider audience through the voice of one of its target customers.

Part two of the plan was called the Glove Box, the brand's on-site activation. Visitors were asked to complete a short personality quiz to determine their SXSW "type" (e.g., newbie), then were e-mailed custom mobile-optimized daily itineraries recommending panels, films, concerts, and other activities. Each itinerary contained a unique scannable QR code that gave participants one chance per day to "unlock" a chance to win prizes contained in a giant, eight-foot Glove Box (where you keep your insurance card, get it?). If a participant unlocked the Glove Box, it lit up in spectacular fashion (revving engine, flickering gauges, shooting steam) to reveal high-end prizes like iPad Minis and Beats by Dre headphones. The entertaining and unexpected prize delivery experience kept participants coming back for more throughout the festival (43 percent of registrants scanned at least twice; 26 percent three times).

The activation earned 295 unique registrations per day and drew 20 to 30 bystanders for each attempt at unlocking the Glove Box. Most importantly, through powerful word-of-mouth, attendees frequently reported seeking out the Esurance Glove Box to sign up because their friends told them to.

Elsewhere, a high-tech facial recognition event kiosk dubbed Face-Look (tied into the Face.com platform) allowed consumers to take photos of themselves and use the images to log in and post directly to Facebook at Coke's Summer Love events.

The technology might best be known to tech-savvy Facebook users as Photo Finder and Photo Tagger, which enables users to quickly find and tag photos of friends on Facebook. But the platform is quickly expanding beyond the confines of the web and into the realm of live events where it's leveraging real-world fun to generate massive social media buzz.

Coca-Cola tested out the technology through a series of "Summer Love" events activated across Israel that targeted teens and utilized the cutting-edge FaceLook app to prove that the 125-year-old brand is anything but old fashioned. Prior to the events, teens registered through Facebook, where they could opt in to use the app. Once they arrived at the event, they could post to their Facebook pages just by looking at a FaceLook kiosk. The app's technology worked like a photo booth. Users began the process with a few taps on the touchscreen kiosk, then were directed to look into the screen as it counted down from three. It then snapped the image, identified the user, and automatically posted a comment or a branded "like" related to the event.

Teens at the Summer Love event could post as many times as they wanted . . . and did they ever. The Summer Love program inspired tens of thousands of people to snap their images and post to Facebook while enjoying the live event. The technology brought teens together and provided an easy and intuitive way for them to share Coca-Cola's message across their vast social networks, generating exponential buzz across Israel and the world.

The FaceLook campaign wasn't Coke's first foray into high-tech Facebook integration. A year before, the brand activated a Coca-Cola

Village experience. Teens were challenged to collect 10 Coca-Cola caps and then bring together eight more teens who did the same in order to register online for exclusive access to the event. At the event, attendees signed up for a wristband that instantly posted the user's status to his or her Facebook page every time the band was swiped at a new on-site activity. The wristband also automatically tagged all the photos taken at the Village. With an ever-expanding soft drink and energy drink market to compete in, Coca-Cola is clearly embracing emerging technologies to win the hearts and minds of its up-and-coming brand loyalists.

Overall, technology has allowed the tenets of experience design to make deeper, more personalized connections. *Example:* For basketball fans who have always wondered what it would be like to shoot hoops with their favorite players, Nike's Air Jordan Flight Lab was a virtual dream come true. The retail experience was unveiled in celebration of the NBA All-Star Weekend in New Orleans, where Nike took over a Footaction store. Press events held in the space throughout the weekend included highlight appearances from Jordan Brand athletes, cultural leaders, and even His Airness himself. But the real action was found inside the lab.

Offering a first-of-its-kind experience, Nike used holographic technology to bring NBA stars to life. The holographic training experience, which served as the lab's primary engagement, allowed consumers to learn signature moves from hyper-realistic holographic athletes, including Carmelo Anthony, Chris Paul, and Blake Griffin (who made a surprise appearance), and then attempt to mimic the maneuvers. Consumers were also invited to create their own models of shoes with the assistance of the brand's design team, and then digitally post them to a large display on the opposite side of the room.

BRINGING BRANDS TO LIFE

Leveraging experience design allows marketing—limited for decades to a paltry two dimensions—to now bust out of its box and make a 3-D connection. And design—too often grounded in mere aesthetics—can now use brand-driven strategy to give form the ultimate function. Fused together, the best of both come alive to form an unstoppable solution that can deliver in any space, in every way.

Chapter Seven Proving Performance and Measurement

One of the biggest challenges marketers face is rationalizing the high perceived cost of experiential marketing relative to other options they have for communicating their messages. For years, marketers relied on gut feelings, previous experience, or more qualitative satisfaction metrics for ROI assessments because more sophisticated measurement tools and methods either didn't exist or produced results that were not projectable. Leads from events were often so unreliable that dealers didn't want them; those from trade shows frequently never made it from marketing to the sales team for follow-up. Consumer survey information, when collected, sometimes wound up in a desk drawer.

To be fair, since the earliest days, most experiential marketers have tried to measure. They collected attendee data pre-event and followed up with post-event surveys. By the early 2000s, they were measuring lead quality and quantity, evaluating their marketing communications messages, calculating sales potential, and tracking media impressions. But as savvy as their instincts may have been, their tactics remained stuck in the Stone Age. Marketers tracked trade show traffic with a clicker at the entrance door. To determine attendance at summer activations, they counted parking spaces in concert venue parking lots. At street fairs, they estimated how many people could fit on a city block—or counted how many cars drove past a promotional vehicle in one minute—then multiplied. The flaw was that, while such data might be of interest, they were virtually useless in assessing how well, let alone if, the campaign delivered on time spent, speed of action, and relationship development.

On a pure "cost-per-touch" basis, there's no doubt that experiential marketing can seem more expensive than other media options. This is because major drivers of cost are the production and logistics needed to support the essential live-event component of an experiential program.

We've heard many CMOs question why they would spend millions of dollars to reach *thousands* of people with an experiential program when they could spend the same amount to reach *millions* via more traditional forms of digital, broadcast, and print media. In fact, a marketing procurement executive at a major package goods company that relies heavily on Sunday coupon inserts to promote its brands made that argument to us a few years ago. It's a legitimate question, and it reveals the lack of any one standard by which to measure the ROI of experiential marketing. We pointed out that if, rather than distributing 50-cent coupons for his company's products and training his customers never to buy at full price, he could spend the same or less to get people to buy at full price *and* become advocates for his brands, then he could potentially create a better business impact.

Marketers who apply the "cost vs. reach" comparison of experiential to other forms of media risk missing out on the true promise of Experiential Marketing, which accomplishes three goals better than any other:

1. Experiential Marketing enables brands to spend more time with their stakeholders. It's the ultimate opt-in strategy because participants elect to invest their time and interact with your brand. "Touching" someone with a passive impression should not be equated to engaging with a stakeholder in a meaningful live interaction. An active engagement is worth more because it leads to the strategy's second goal;

2. Experiential Marketing requires less time to inspire action. Engagement fosters better understanding of your product or service benefits and how the brand fits into the customer's lifestyle, and it lowers

the barriers for trial and purchase. All of this combines to minimize risk and accelerate conversion, which increases your chances not only for short-term action, but for one of Experiential Marketing's most powerful goals;

3. Experiential Marketing leads to longer relationships and advocacy that pay off over time. Loyalty is achieved when a brand delivers on its promises. Advocacy occurs when the promise is combined with an experience that compels your customers to share with their friends, their families, and with wider social or business networks.

So shouldn't experiential marketing be measured based on its ability to create and accelerate short- and long-term business outcomes rather than on how much it costs to "touch" each person? The answer is yes. Cost metrics are important for benchmarking and planning purposes, but they are only one stroke on a much larger canvas.

It's the event that provides the context and the content that are critical in motivating your stakeholders to discover, understand, purchase, and evangelize your brand. And yet it is the biggest obstacle to cost-justification. Events have become, after advertising, the second-largest expenditure for marketers, according to the EMI/Mosaic Experiential Marketing 2015 Event Track Report. Marketers still believe they produce the highest returns. And today they have the tools to support their case. With sophisticated data capture and analysis tools, marketers can assess not only how many attendees came to an event, but when they registered, their gender, age, purchase intent, and more. The technology exists to track an attendee's digital body language as well as his or her event body language; to measure new leads and client retention; sales revenue; sales growth; and a customer's lifetime value. Add to this list net promoter scores, brand awareness levels, social media sharing, and press coverage. You name it, and someone can measure it.

Driving this move toward more sophisticated forms of measurement is that advances in technology are shifting the marketing function at many companies from a focus on branding and awareness to lead generation and financial impact. At Microsoft, for example, marketers are being encouraged by management to move away from looking at pure ROI as a measure of success or failure, and to instead focus on the impact of their efforts on the company's specific business objectives. For a company that produces more than 10,000 events around the world each year, this is a signal that experiential marketing has moved from tactic to strategy.

Events and experiential marketing have always excelled at increasing awareness, building brands, and generating high-quality leads. And experiential marketers have always *believed* in the ROI of their efforts. Trade shows, meetings and conferences, sponsorships, mobile tours, even sampling programs all have the ability to engage stakeholders as they are seeking information, are about to make a purchase, or when they're just looking for a taste of something new.

The good news for marketers is that telling a persuasive story about the power of experiential marketing is getting easier, and recent Event Marketing Institute research (2015) shows that more marketers are measuring their experiential programs. In fact, continuing a trend, 79 percent of brands reported measuring their experiential programs in 2015, up from 71 percent in 2013. The top measurement factors and criteria that marketers are focusing on are total attendance, social media activity, and number of sales leads. What's more, brands that measure their experiential marketing programs are two-thirds more likely to see increased budgets for experiential. See Figure 7.1.

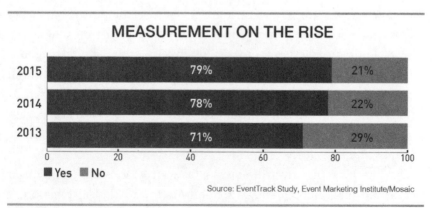

FIGURE 7.1   More Marketers Are Measuring

METRICS THAT MATTER

Once you've established clear and measurable goals, you can use the following metrics to determine whether they have been achieved. Your goal should be to assemble the right group of metrics for your situation and use them to gather not only quantitative returns, but just as importantly, key insights on customer behavior that can inform future business decisions and marketing strategy.

- *Attendee Demographics.* Event marketers have always counted heads. Now you can track when and how attendees registered, which in turn reveals valuable information about which promotions and registration methods are working best. Are the attendees responding to an ad, a tweet, e-mail, or a referral from a friend? Knowing who is attending also matters. Is the attendee a decision-maker with purchase power, a top sales person, or just someone tagging along for the ride? Remember, it's not just a numbers game anymore.
- *Satisfaction.* What is their perception of the event? Was it meaningful? Will they return next year? Should you change the event or eliminate it from your marketing portfolio?
- *Mindshare.* How did the event move the needle on brand awareness and knowledge? Will the attendee buy your product or service? Recommend it to others? Does the attendee even remember who sponsored the event?
- *Journey.* Which sessions, content, interactives, and product demos did the participant attend? Did he or she comment in chat rooms or on social media?
- *Sales Leads.* Quality counts. Determine which attendees wield the buying power and know their position in the sales funnel.
- *Acquisition Cost.* Like sales leads, this metric is necessary to determine just how much time, effort, and expense go into acquiring actual customers and the cost to retain them and increase their purchases.
- *Lifetime Value.* Measuring the sales value of an attendee over a period of time versus someone who didn't attend reveals the impact of the event or conference on the bottom line and shows that the relationships that develop from those events lead to more significant lifetime value.

- *Revenue and Sales Growth.* For many meetings and events, it's all about the bottom line. Make sure it increases year over year and track spikes in relationship to event activations.
- *ROI.* Measuring return on investment requires that you know what your business value is minus your costs, and it reveals what marketers are getting for those dollars.
- *Event Body Language.* This registers attendees' activity at an event, including which sessions or interactives they attend. For example, knowing whether they attended high-level, industry thought leadership sessions or skipped those in favor of training on specific products or tools allows for better post-event follow-up.
- *Digital Body Language.* Measures attendees' online activity, which may begin with an e-mail, a website visit, the download of an event-associated white paper, a post to a social media site, and so on. Digital body language reveals whether an attendee is in a shopping mindset or an advocacy mindset, which can help you tailor your follow-up accordingly.
- *Communications.* How effective are your marketing messages? Are they connecting your brand with your audience?
- *Press Impact.* Unpaid media is a common objective of experiential programs. How many media mentions did your program rack up? Which editors and publications? Calculate what the cost would have been to reach those audiences with paid advertising equivalent to the time and space you got for free and put a dollar value on the media reach of your program. Also important to look at is whether the coverage you received was positive or negative, and to what extent any coverage conveyed the key points you wanted to communicate with your program.
- *Social Media Buzz.* Facebook, Twitter, YouTube, and Pinterest all represent social currency that should be measured in terms of likes, tweets, fans, and followers.
- *Advocacy.* Are your participants sharing your content or promoting your message to their networks? Is what they're sharing positive or negative? Does the content of their communications sync with the messaging of your campaign? How quickly are they spreading the word, and to how many people? How many of the second-tier people

have now engaged with your brand? Do you know? By building sharable content into your experiential campaigns, you can claim the "follow on" interactions among those who you didn't "touch" directly to augment your direct engagements and bring down the cost-per-touch of your program.

Example: If I engaged with 20,000 people live and online, and 25 percent (5,000 people) of my audience shared content (videos, photos, special offers) with their social networks, allowing my message to reach an additional 20,000 people, then my cost-per-touch can be cut in half.

- *Sales Impact.* Did participation lead to measurable sales, and over what period of time? Establish a half-life benchmark for your events to capture purchases and claim credit. You can do this by monitoring sales in bands that make sense for your brand—ranging from days to weeks to months to years. In order to prove the connection between the experience and sale, you'll need to have captured the participants' identifying information and ensure that you have visibility into sales data.

- *Sales Potential.* What percentage of those who engaged have purchased in the past? Use this data as a benchmark for future projections. If you know that 40 percent of those who take a certain number of actions—attended an event, shared your content, and so on—ultimately made a purchase in the past, then use that benchmark as you scale up/down your experiences, and to justify your budgets.

- *Sales Velocity.* How quickly after the experience did the prospect purchase? Getting people to buy is great. Getting them to buy more quickly generates exponentially more revenue for your company.

- *Speed to Action.* Did the participant take one or more actions: downloaded information; shared your content online; visited your website? More importantly, can you connect those initial actions to later purchases?

- *Net Promoter Score.* Net Promoter Scores are calculated using the answer to a single question: *How likely is it that you would recommend [brand name] to a friend or colleague?* Respondents are grouped along a 10-point scale based on their answers:
  - *Promoters (score 9 to 10).* Loyal enthusiasts who will continue to buy and will refer others, creating growth.

○ *Passives (score 7 to 8).* Satisfied but not enthusiastic customers who can be enticed to switch brands.

○ *Detractors (score 0 to 6).* Unhappy customers who can damage your brand and stifle growth through negative word-of-mouth.

To determine your Net Promoter Score, subtract the percentage of Detractors from the percentage of Promoters. Your score can range from a low of −100 (if every customer is a Detractor) to a high of +100 (if every customer is a Promoter). Net Promoter was introduced by Fred Reichheld in a 2004 *Harvard Business Review* article, based on research done with Satmetrix. The research identified a link between higher Net Promoter Scores and business growth.

• **Message Retention:** Did attendees leave your experience able to recall and retell your story—or at least the main messages you were trying to communicate? This metric can be useful in evaluating internal events such as sales meetings.

Example: If a sales rep fully understands the features and benefits of your new product after having participated in a sales event, and that new product represents potentially $50 million in sales for your company, then his or her chances of making a business impact should be better than that of a peer who did not fully internalize the messaging. In this scenario you could assign a dollar value (e.g., by using a sales quota) to represent the value of message retention (and conversely, the cost to the company for each rep who is unable to sell the benefits of the new product).

• *Loyalty.* Did the experience increase the likelihood that customers will buy in the future? Net Promoter Score is one way to measure loyalty. Other ways include tracking sales data over time.

• *Viral Activity.* Did participants share your message or content with their friends, families, or social networks? Viral activity should be built into every campaign because peer-to-peer sharing is more likely to create follow-on engagement among indirect participants who act on recommendations from their friends. You can also use the viral reach of your campaign to reduce your cost-per-touch.

• *Time Spent.* How much time did participants spend with you? The number is meaningless unless you've predetermined a goal for the optimal experience and then created your program around that.

Example: Several years ago Southern Comfort created a brand experience tour and determined that 12 minutes was the right amount of time to give consumers a walk-through journey of the brand's heritage in a converted trailer. For a more complex product like a medical diagnostic device, the optimal time spent might be two hours.

- *Marketing Channel Impact.* How did the experiential program impact other parts of the marketing mix? These could include downloads, web traffic, app interactives, microsite activity, and so on.
- *Purchase intent.* Are participants more or less likely to purchase your product or service after the experience?

These are the primary areas that experiential marketers focus on. But few care about all of them. Your goal should be to select the metrics that make sense for your own situation and, where possible, use the same metrics across all of your events so that you can build benchmarks for future activities. Your chosen metrics will become key performance indicators and should be a mix of quantitative and qualitative measures that are important to three constituencies: (1) for marketing managers to justify expenditures, create benchmarks for future performance, and improve the experience for participants; (2) for senior marketing management to compare with other channels of marketing being used and to assess movement in brand perception and business impact; and (3) for financial managers to monitor ROI.

Over time, you will use your metrics not just to grade each program, but more importantly, to begin to gain insights into customer behavior that can inform other areas of your business, from product development to pricing and more.

BUILDING YOUR PERFORMANCE PLAN

There are so many ways that experiential marketing can impact your business that there is no "one way" to measure its impact. The best approach is to understand what it is you want to achieve with your experiential program. Is it short-term sales? Long-term sales? Awareness? Advocacy? Relationship enhancement? Some of these? All of these? Once you have consensus around your business objectives, then it's time to build a program designed to effect the outcomes you want, along with a measurement strategy that is relevant for your situation. By taking this "ground up" approach to measurement, you'll be able to determine the return on your experiential marketing investment by focusing on the outcome you hope to achieve, not just the costs to achieve it. Once you have determined which metrics are right for your situation, be sure to apply them to every campaign moving forward. Your goal should be to establish a set of benchmarks that can be used to plan and monitor your programs in the future.

Because there is no "right" way to measure experiential marketing, the following are a variety of examples of how leading advocates of the strategy are approaching measurement within their organizations and for their programs. We present these as models that you can use as inspiration to create your own criteria for proving the performance of your experiential campaigns.

The Economics of Time

More experiential marketing pros are taking their measurement and analysis to the next level and creating "power indexes" of sorts that roll their data into models that add dimension to the stats.

Jack Morton Worldwide, one of the largest experiential marketing agencies, uses the data it collects from client programs to create a story around both the time economics of experiential ROI and how quickly audiences move through the purchase funnel.

For time economics, the company looks at the following:

- Rate of audience acquisition and retention
- Speed to action and performance
- Speed to purchase
- Customer lifetime value
- Customer referral value

For purchase velocity, the company measures the following:

- *Awareness:* number of people exposed; increase in recall and understanding

- *Consideration:* increase in reported "fit" with beliefs and actions; change in perception
- *Preference:* increase in perceived relevance; agreement with messaging; positive differentiation; intent to purchase
- *Commitment:* increase in aligned attitudes and behaviors; intent to learn more about the brand; increase in belief/trust; purchase
- *Advocacy:* positive word-of-mouth recommendation; number of advocates; number of people acting on recommendations; Net Promoter Score

Here is how this measurement strategy was applied to an automotive brand for which the agency created a multi-city tour with nearly 15,000 participants.

More Time Spent with Consumers
- Sixty-three percent of consumers participating spent between 16 and 60 minutes learning about the car and talking to brand ambassadors about it.
- Ten percent spent more than 60 minutes.
- Time spent with the brand rose at stops where there was more interactivity with the product.

Less Time Between Awareness and Purchase
- Forty-three percent of consumers arrived with little or no prior awareness of the car.
- Forty-nine percent left the experience extremely or very likely to purchase the car in the future.
- Thirteen percent were in the market to purchase within three months.

Long-Term Payoff
- Participants had a Net Promoter Score of 49 (16 is considered average).
- According to a model for likely word-of-mouth behavior established by Walter J. Carl of Northeastern University, the 56 percent of participants who qualified as "passionates" because they responded to the

recommendation question with a 9 or 10 had a likelihood of creating an additional 400,000 experiential impressions through positive word of mouth.

Clearly, measurement criteria were built into this experiential program from the start. The brand doesn't make the mistake of trying to measure after the program is in motion, or worse, after the campaign has ended.

THE POWER OF TOUCH

For marketers whose products are sold in retail stores, best-in-class experiential programs engage shoppers and provide opportunities to drive sales, equity, and loyalty at the same time. Building bigger, more immersive experiential marketing events will be a critical pillar to building brands at retail and helping retailers drive stronger shopper traffic, notes Carl Preller, chief performance officer at Geometry Global, a large experiential marketing agency that creates and manages thousands of in-store marketing programs each year.

Here is how Geometry Global approaches measurement of its clients' in-store experiential programs (Figure 7.2).

1. Think Shopper Journey
   ○ Redefining the role of experiential marketing within shopper marketing needs to be grounded in understanding its role across the shopper decision journey. Geometry Global research into shopper decision journeys shows that in many grocery categories experiential marketing is often both the *least* utilized tactic and the *most* influential one.
   ○ The implications of this insight suggest that marketers need to understand and measure experiential tactics in the context of a shopper journey both with, and against, the variety of other communication channels at their disposal. Likewise, it is clear that there is strong evidence that brands should be rethinking how much investment they are putting into experiential as a critical part of their marketing mix. Marketers are always making

Percentage of Shoppers who experience an event of some sort

Percentage of Shoppers who rate experiential events as highly influential

Hispanic Shopper — 11% — 32%

Millennials — 10% — 20%

Gen X — 12% — 21%

Boomers — 7% — 17%

FIGURE 7.2   Consumer Survey: The Impact of Experiences
Source: Geometry Global

choices and measurement can and should play a role in their deci-sion-making process.

2. Think "Clicks to Bricks"

   ○ There is a second implication when thinking in terms of shop-per journeys versus "events." The very best experiential programs build the shopper experience across multiple local communication channels, including social and mobile that begin well before your first in-person contact.

   ○ Your marketing mix choices need to be driven by comparing tactic efficiencies as well as understanding how tactics working together can help build a bigger, more impactful program.

3. Think "Return on Involvement" Versus "Return on Investment."
   - Experiential programs are often considered expensive, and bad ones certainly can be, notes Preller. The truth, however, is often driven by the way marketers look at their programs. Great experiential programming is high touch and high impact. These are activities that are designed to drive long-term brand equity and loyalty, and your experiential scorecard should be able to capture the value you continue to receive after an event. ROI measurement should give your experiential programs "fair credit" for the sales and loyalty they generate in the post-event period (see the Measurement Windows chart on page 153). To do this you need to ensure you understand what Preller calls the "true sales incrementality" you receive from your events both during and after the event:
   - Brand Sales Incrementality = incremental sales during and post-event
   - Brand Return on Involvement = Incremental sales during/post, less program costs

Measuring Shopper Impact

You can measure shopper impact by assessing brand awareness and engagement lift, "shopper incrementality," and the "shopper share of voice" that your programs create:

- *Brand Awareness and Loyalty.* Understand how your programs contribute to awareness and engagement.
- *Shopper Incrementality.* This is typically assessed via loyalty card data. This measure is important to understand how events drive new shoppers to your brand and/or persuade current loyal shoppers to buy more.

Measuring Path-to-Purchase Impact

To fully assess the impact of your retail-based experiential programs, you need to understand how they perform in the context of the overall path to purchase. Geometry Global looks at the following key metrics when assessing the performance of its clients' programs:

- *Shopper Impressions*. Gauge the actual level of impressions your programs drive in the context of the entire marketing plan.
- *Sales Attribution*. Similar to Brand Sales Incrementality, this metric measures the sales contribution directly tied to the experiential activation compared to other tactics that are part of the marketing mix.

BRANDS MAKING HEADWAY

Activision's approach to measurement is also instructive. The company behind the wildly successful Call of Duty video game franchise could have spent tens of millions of marketing dollars to saturate the airwaves to reach millions of its target audience around the world to promote the launch of the latest version of the game in 2011. Instead, the company spent a few million dollars to bring its online world to life for only 6,000 of its most loyal customers.

Call of Duty: XP immersed fans in Modern Warfare 3. At the time it was the latest game in the popular Activision Call of Duty series. Activision literally brought the game to life with a two-day experience that pitted attendees against each other in real-life contests and electronic gameplay (for a more complete look at this program, see Chapter 4).

The program set a new bar for experiential fan-based events and became the first entertainment launch in history to reach $1 billion in sales.

A traditional marketer would look at a multi-million-dollar spend that "touched" only 6,000 participants and call it a waste of money. After all, think of how many millions of customers could be reached by applying the same spend to digital and broadcast media. But Activision used the event to galvanize the most rabid of their fans and unleash *them* as the channel that would propagate their message around the world.

Activision focused on the outcome, not the cost, and they were able to track purchases, speed of purchase tied to various campaign activations; and—because this was the equivalent of a movie launch—the cost of impressions compared to a paid media buy.

Another company seeing positive returns is Chrysler, where a favorite form of activation remains the test drive. Data helps Chrysler measure where it has been and target where to go next to optimize consumers' time and its own investment in its portfolio of activations, activities, and engagement points. The company deploys a standard survey that asks attendees—in addition to vehicle-specific information—a core set of questions, including how they feel about the brand and permission to contact them in the future. The format can be either paper or electronic. Post-activity, the company asks how attendees feel about the brand. After having implemented a consistent measurement strategy over several years, the company has amassed a robust set of data that allows Chrysler's marketers to monitor key success indicators such as time in market, gender, age—even whether a participant is a current customer (which could trigger a loyalty offer) or an owner of a competitive brand (which could trigger a conquest offer). The company is also using its benchmark data to determine which types of events they should be at, including the time of year, location, and lifestyle programming most likely to yield the best results.

Surveys still play an important role in measuring effectiveness at Cisco's Global Sales Experience (GSX), the company's annual global internal sales meeting that attracts upwards of 20,000 attendees and is beamed across 72 locations around the globe over a period of four days. Measurement has always been critical to Cisco, but over the past few years it has evolved from metrics around how many people attended events, speaker ratings, and attendee satisfaction scores to measuring business impact. Interviewed by *Event Marketer* (2014), Alex Sapiz, senior director-sales and partner engagements and recognition at Cisco, told us: "Our events have to move the needle in terms of our ability to help our sellers grow, accelerate, and win business. We needed to go much deeper in terms of understanding our impact, and that understanding only comes from looking at the data in a very disciplined way."

Cisco begins the process by asking attendees a basic question: Do you believe that this event is helping you grow, accelerate, and win business? The day after GSX closes, Cisco sends out a more extensive online survey. Researchers analyze that data and produce a 20-slide executive summary that details where GSX most effectively touched its audience.

That post-event survey led to the finding in 2012 that the top 10 percent of its sellers felt they weren't getting enough recognition at GSX. "Because we look at the segmentation and demographics, we are able to slice and dice the data and understand that not all audiences are created equal," said Sapiz. Based on the information from that survey, Sapiz built a business case for creating a program to address the lack of recognition for that 10 percent. By the following year the satisfaction gap had disappeared.

GSX is an internal event where confidential information is disclosed to the sales force, so social media that goes outside of the Cisco TV platform is prohibited. But for consumer-facing events, the more social the better, in terms of data mining.

LEGO supported the relaunch of its Star Wars sets with an integrated program that measured not only sales, but customer lifetime value as well. The campaign involved the Cartoon Network and its "Yoda Chronicles" property, along with retail and digital components. Called Secrets to Reveal There Are, the campaign focused on a big moment in Times Square where LEGO would reveal a secret. Kids and their parents were encouraged to visit LEGO stores or use their LEGOs at home to build whatever they thought the secret might be. They entered photos of their creations into a sweepstakes-like contest on a microsite, becoming part of a digital nurturing stream in which the company could continue to engage with them leading up to the big reveal. Fans could download a Yoda Chronicles mobile app, search out secrets through YouTube videos, and check for hints during spots that ran on the Cartoon Network.

Key performance indicators revealed that 66 percent of consumers unfamiliar with the Yoda Chronicles were aware of it by the end of the campaign; 56 percent said they were likely to purchase LEGOs after the event; and 90 percent said they would share the experience with friends and family. Retail events and digital activity drove a 3 percent increase in sales, and the company saw a 43 percent rise in sales of the LEGO Star Wars line month-over-month after the event, a valuable measure of customer lifetime value.

THE NEXT PHASE

At Microsoft—which over the course of the last eight years has systematically transformed its event and experiential footprint from thousands of unconnected events run by different teams into a more streamlined and strategically driven event and experiential strategy—measurement has become an institutionalized part of every conversation.

Historically, Microsoft measured the success of its events by looking primarily at attendee satisfaction scores. The team would combine its post-event survey results with a few budget metrics to assign a value to the program. But the data wasn't helping the team tell a very good story. The concept for a consistent measurement tool was brought to the team from one of its European subsidiaries and was executed at U.S. head-quarters in two phases: first, the team standardized the metrics so that it could compare data across events, apples to apples; second, they created one central repository to hold all of the information.

"We based [the tool] on our marketing objectives for the company," recalls Kati Quigley, who heads up Microsoft's largest event, the World-wide Partner Conference (WPC). "We looked overall and said, 'these are our six marketing objectives for the company that we care about, no mat-ter what kind of marketing we're doing.' We can feed into that and say, 'This is how [our team] touches and affects those marketing objectives.' I think it continues to make the case that events are a strong marketing vehicle." To standardize the metrics, the team merges traditional cost-per-head metrics and satisfaction data into an overall satisfaction score. Then, the tool combines those scores with new metrics that are tied to the company's return on marketing investment (ROMI) objectives.

A weighting system gives more value to the ROMI scores so the event staff can get a more accurate picture of how the event did in terms of marketing strategy versus attendee perception. The tool requires anyone initiating an event program to select primary and secondary marketing objectives as part of a pre-program briefing, building more accountability into the process and putting event managers in a more strategic role as consultants and advisors to the business owners they work with. "It's a conversation with that busi-ness team, but we're driving it," says group event marketing manager Jenny Laidlaw, who heads up the initiative. "It's something our team can bring for-ward to say, 'Hey, we have these ROMI objectives as a company. Let's make sure your event objectives tie in to that.' We're asking questions so at the end of the event we can actually tell you if you were successful."

PRACTICE MEASUREMENT DISCIPLINE

All the emphasis on data and measurement can be overwhelming, and it may be tempting to take a "measure everything you can" mentality. But just because you *can* measure something doesn't mean you should.

A simpler approach, and one that can provide better insights versus more data, is to organize your metrics under three headings: Financial Performance, which looks at all of your "cost-per" data and ROI metrics; Benchmarks, which are the key performance indicators that are meaningful to your team and/or management; and Insights, which allow you to fine-tune your program and ensure that you are optimizing your ability to create meaningful business impact.

However you go about it, metrics must relate directly to the goals you establish for your program or campaign. Cisco, for example, sets out its goals for GSX a full 12 months in advance, and everything is designed to track back to the goals and the strategy set forward when the team starts the planning cycle.

MEASUREMENT TRENDS

More companies are measuring their event and experiential programs, and they are using a wider range of tracking metrics and approaches.

ROI Expectations

Events and experiences provide a significant ROI. The survey asked specifically: What ROI do you expect from events? Forty-eight percent of brands realize an ROI of between 3:1 to 5:1, and 29 percent indicated their return is over 10:1. Twelve percent say their ROI is 20:1 or higher. (See Figure 7.3.)

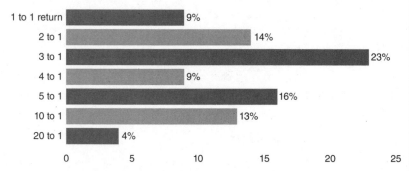

Figure 7.3   Average ROI: Experiential Marketing
Source: EMI/Mosaic EventTrack 2015

Continued

Continued

	2012%	2013%	2014%	2015%
Attendance/participation	74%	83%	80%	85%
Social media postings/followings/shares	45%	37%	57%	61%
Leads	62%	67%	64%	58%
Post-experience overall sales	46%	49%	66%	57%
P.R./media coverage	56%	54%	59%	47%
Web traffic	41%	50%	46%	47%
Experiential campaign's gross sales	49%	54%	32%	47%
On-site sales	31%	29%	41%	44%
Time spent at experience	31%	25%	34%	44%
Other online/mobile activities	29%	26%	30%	30%
Retail shelf lifts	na	na	9%	18%
Gross profit related to campaign	24%	30%	32%	na
Other metrics	11%	5%	9%	5%

Figure 7.4   Performance Criteria
Source: EMI/Mosaic EventTrack 2015

Performance Criteria

The top measurement factors and criteria marketers are using to judge performance are total attendance, Facebook and social media activity, and number of leads. (See Figure 7.4.)

	2013%	2014%	2015%
On-site surveys or interviews	47%	59%	65%
Post-event surveys or interviews	65%	64%	64%
Interactive technology tracking tools	na	15%	42%
Redemptions of incentives	24%	49%	36%
RFID/NFC tracking	na	18%	19%
Other	8%	3%	8%

Figure 7.5   Measurement Methods
Source: EMI/Mosaic EventTrack 2015

Measurement Methods

The main measurement methods are on-site surveys or interviews, post-event surveys, and interactive technology tracking tools. Nineteen percent of brands are using RFID or Near Field Communication (NFC) tracking as part of their measurement process today. (See Figure 7.5.)

Measurement Windows

Sixty-six percent of brands conduct their measurement process within three months after the event or experiential program. Thirty percent measure within a six-month post-event window and 27 percent measure within a full-year period. Note, the percentages add to over 100 percent as many brands measure various events and experiential programs on different timelines. (See Figure 7.6.)

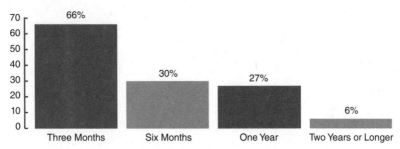

Figure 7.6   Measurement Windows
Source: EMI/Mosaic EventTrack 2015

REFERENCES

EMI/Mosaic Experiential Marketing. (2015). Event track report. *Event Marketer*, April 2014.
Jack Morton Worldwide. (2008). White paper. New York: Jack Morton Worldwide.
Reichheld, F. (2004). Motivating through metrics. *Harvard Business Review*. www .netpromoter.com

Chapter Eight   The 10 Habits of Highly Experiential Brands

People often ask us which brands create the best experiences and which most effectively use experiential marketing.

There isn't a single brand that excels above all others. But there are certainly many that have "cracked the code" and are using live experiences as the driver of an integrated mix that connects, engages, and converts. In many cases, harnessing the incredible power of experiential marketing required marketers to rewire their strategies—to accept and understand that what has worked for their companies for the last 25 years won't work for the next 25.

Nobody has studied and been given access to more experiential marketing strategies and programs than we have. And through that access we've discovered four Common Strategic Traits shared among highly successful users of brand experiences.

- *Dependency on Strategy.* Brands develop and leverage a specific road map for achieving goals with experiential marketing.
- *Balanced Mix.* Brand experiences are connected to the rest of the marketing mix, often used as the lead driver of strategy or lead provider of content.

- *Definitive Target.* A well-defined and isolated target audience is identified and engaged via experiential marketing. (Many of our friends in the industry have heard us joke for years that, "18 to 55 is not a target audience. It's the human race.")
- *Bold Ideas.* A lack of fear and a willingness to take risk are absolutely key to the successful use of experience engagement. In a discipline that brings brands to life, big ideas reign supreme.

Beyond the Common Strategic Traits, we've analyzed thousands of experiential programs to uncover what makes them tick, or the DNA of successful brand experiences. When we compare and contrast brand experiences, we see that there are 10 specific habits shared by the best users of experiential marketing.

THE DNA OF EXPERIENCES

Habit 10. Focus on Driving Trial

Use experiential marketing to create longer engagements that promote the test, sample, or demonstration of a product or service. Key tips:

- *Embrace Acceleration.* Trial speeds up purchase intent. When a target tries a product, movement toward the top of the purchase funnel accelerates.
- *Go Beyond a Sample.* Smart marketers are moving beyond simply handing a customer a sample and instead are creating an experience around the engagement of trying the product.
- *Design Longer Trials.* Our own studies show that a longer engagement equals a deeper experience. Successful users of experiential marketing are creating programs that generate longer conversations and engagements with targets.
- *Measure Sales Lift.* Trial programs are some of the most measureable experiences. Successful marketers have processes in place to record and benchmark real-time sales movement.

Example: To elevate its "Make Moments Happen" marketing messaging in a live setting, and build momentum for a new in-store promotion and ad campaign, Nestlé activated a trial experience at Bayside Market-place in Miami with a surprise-and-delight twist.

Brand ambassadors handed out samples made with Nescafé Clásico to passersby and asked, "Would you have a cup of Nescafé Clásico with a perfect stranger?" Consumers who accepted and entered the footprint were invited to sit, sip (on iced or hot coffee), and hang out with other consumers in the lounge. There were crowd-driven ice-breaker games, including Iced-Coffee-Breaker Bingo, where attendees would work with each other to answer trivia questions. In a branded photo booth, consumers were encouraged to snap photos and share them via #MomentoNescafé.

Consumers who completed the games and shared images were given a Nescafé Clásico branded tumbler and samples of the product, as well as an iced coffee recipe to take home. Some consumers, however, were treated to a celebrity surprise. Brand ambassadors handpicked extra-eager consumers and invited them into an air-conditioned tent with a stylish waiting area. Once inside, special guest singer Ricky Martin, current spokesperson for the brand, popped in to surprise them and chat over a mug of Nescafé Clásico. Nestlé filmed the surprises with Ricky Martin to use on its social media channels and in commercial spots.

Habit 9. Make It Unforgettable—Literally

The target won't (and can't) forget the experience and is able to relive it and reshare it for days, weeks, and years.

- *Create a Memory.* Build experiences with elements in place that allow the target audience to re-experience the experience.
- *Stoke the Relationship.* Design the experience around the goal of using long-term "experiential recall" to develop a long-term relationship.
- *Break the Clutter.* Be conscious of what other brands are doing and develop the brand experience to rise above any category, market, or event clutter that is in place.
- *Use Digital Tools.* Build in tools and platforms—apps, social media platforms, viral videos—that will help consumers relive the experience and stay in contact with the brand.

Example: Truck manufacturer Freightliner proved that the world really is a stage by turning the iconic Hoover Dam into a colossal projection screen to debut its newest vehicle to approximately 200 media members and other influencers.

Using projection-mapping technology, the brand set the dam's 420,000-square-foot surface ablaze with 60 projectors which, at 26,000 watts each, produced 1.17 million lumens (equivalent to the light output of 1,400 60-watt light bulbs) and shattered the Guinness World Record for highest light output projection. Not impressed yet? Consider this: the size of the dam's usable surface is the equivalent of 87 average-size IMAX screens or about nine football fields, excluding the end zones.

As a means of promoting its Inspiration Truck—a new, fully autonomous driving tractor-trailer (and the first ever licensed to drive on public roads)—Freightliner used the dam to display an audiovisual presentation that highlighted the history of the company and its milestones. The exhibition culminated with the debut of the actual vehicle, which made a dramatic drive onto the Hoover Dam from the mountains above.

Habit 8. When Something Works, Don't Do It Again

The best brands resist the temptation to repeat experiential marketing campaigns.

- *Forget the "Save As."* Too many marketers simply repeat their experiences—but target audiences are less inclined to engage in the same experience twice.
- *Tweak and Refresh.* Learning what works and what doesn't is key to refreshing and refining ongoing experiences.
- *Understand the ROI.* Analyzing the experience should also provide insights into what specific elements of a program stimulate sales—marketers can then increase usage of those elements in future campaigns.
- *Connect the Campaigns.* The most successful year-after-year experiences are designed to be connected, fielded as fresh and stand-alone engagements, but in a way that reminds the target of past experiences.

Example: Cisco in 2010 set out to save costs by taking its weeklong annual sales meeting, the Global Sales Experience (GSX), out of the real world and into a virtual one for the first time in its 20-year history. That 100 percent virtual meeting experience taught the tech giant several valuable lessons about what works and what doesn't when it comes to educating and motivating a driven and competitive sales force in a non-physical space.

A year later, the Cisco event team reviewed feedback surveys, login reports, and other metrics to understand what worked and what didn't in the completely virtual b-to-b experience. The first lesson? The environment (the actual event interface people interacted with online) and the augmented reality game called "Threshold" (used to "gamify" the online meeting) were top-performing elements. But what the attendees struggled with was staring at eight hours' worth of live content every day, and missing out on the real face-to-face interactions and recognition elements they had looked forward to at previous (live) events.

The team set out to address those issues and improve on the areas that worked well. Step one was to make the event more of a hybrid engagement that leveraged online and live events, with local Cisco offices hosting group sessions via its proprietary TelePresence video conference technology. The local events mostly addressed the recognition concerns, helping local executives and managers to showcase and reward superstar salespeople in front of their colleagues.

The virtual environment was a huge hit in the previous year, with attendees almost universally calling it "stunning" and "beautiful," so exceeding that mark was a new challenge. To raise the bar even further, for the following year's GSX the team brought in internationally recognized architects and graphic designers from all over the world. Using Cisco products to facilitate global collaboration, they designed the new environment, which resembled a utopian fantasy dreamscape.

The gamification was also tweaked. While the Threshold game was a big hit, it may have been too much of a good thing. The post-event analysis revealed that the hyper-competitive sales force was so set on winning the game that they were spending more time looking for the next clue or puzzle for the game and less on the content. Obviously, this was a problem when it came time to meet educational goals. But the game did drive engagement, so to keep what worked and not lose attendee focus, a new game dubbed "The Hunt" was scaled back and kept separate from the main event. (It was still tied to Cisco product information and technology, so it remained an effective educational tool–just not as integrated.)

Other gaming tools included head-to-head Sudoku challenges and the "Togetherizer," a music mash-up software that allowed players to upload a sound clip that would then be "mashed" with other players' sounds to make a new piece of music. They were all archived for players to listen to at their leisure.

To keep the messaging consistent and facilitate the collaborative nature of GSX under the theme of "Together We Can," Cisco designed and built a custom internal social media platform known as the Together App, which the sales force could install on their mobile devices and access via the virtual environment. They posted learnings and comments from sessions and collaborated on session discussions via the platform, which continues to exist within the company's intranet. It was also a vehicle for checking into sessions and filling out evaluation surveys. To showcase and encourage attendees' community spirit, Cisco integrated volunteer opportunities into GSX and donated $100,000 to community charities on behalf of the Cisco sales force.

Habit 7. Design for Screens

Create experiences with device interaction in mind.

- *Connectivity.* Provide opportunities for targets to participate and engage the experience using their devices.
- *Interactive Control.* High-tech activities stimulate longer engagements and often stimulate experiences that can be both shared and shareable.
- *Remote Viewers.* Allow audiences not physically on-site to connect or view experiences. Smart marketers design the experience with those viewers in mind.
- *Screen Jumpers.* Incentivize targets to engage with different experience elements on different devices.

Example: As lead sponsor of Taylor Swift's The 1989 World Tour, XFINITY, Comcast cable's residential service brand, activated touchpoints designed to provide fans with exclusive content on-site as well as at home. The company created an XFINITY Zone at concert venues in select markets it services. The experience promoted the brand's products including the X1 entertainment operating system and the new XR11 voice command remote control that used voice to access TV features. The anchor was an interactive Magic Mirror that let fans speak into a voice remote to engage in a video greeting from the seven-time Grammy winner herself on the two-way mirror. XFINITY customized the demo so that when fans uttered commands, they received a fun, cheeky response from Swift.

In addition, consumers could have their images superimposed next to Swift's via an augmented reality overlay, a photo they could then share on social media or take home—but with a catch. Fans couldn't see her in the photo until it was texted or e-mailed—a share was required. Once XFINITY customers got home they could access exclusive Taylor Swift content On Demand. It all included behind-the-scenes tour footage, interviews, and music videos. To boot, fans who already had the voice remote at home would hear Taylor Swift's voice from the TV, commenting on selections they made. XFINITY referred to the strategy as a couch-to-concert experience. As Taylor Swift fans enjoyed the content, XFINITY was able to compare all of the content being viewed On Demand and measure and determine customer preferences.

Habit 6. Bring the Product to Life

Use live experiences to do what no ad ever could.

- *Translate Features.* Design experiences that give meaning to the attributes of a product.
- *Transaction Staging.* Include opportunities to purchase the product within the experience.
- *Participation = Understanding.* The more participatory the experience, the better the target's understanding will be of the brand, product, or service.
- *Keep It Simple.* The audience has a limited capacity for recall—resist the urge to tell them too much and instead focus on bringing to life the key messages or points.

Example: To promote itself as the best option to fly from New York to Amsterdam (and beyond), KLM Royal Dutch Airlines hosted a three-day pop-up experience at which the airline set out to put its personal and cultural stamp on the air travel experience, targeting consumers and press, plus corporate and VIP guests via private events.

Experiences included a four-hour live art installation by Dutch artist Merijn Hos, who created KLM-inspired illustrations on posters that consumers took home each day. Consumers could listen to Dutch DJs and artists from a private listening booth that helped bring KLM's music sponsorships to life. (KLM is the official carrier of the "World's Best DJs," sponsor of DJ Hardwell's world tour, and sponsor of the EDM Sensation Music Festival in Amsterdam.) Each day starting at 5 p.m., the pop-up transformed into a club with Dutch DJs Regino, Aleppo, and JoeySuki spinning beats.

KLM partnered with Heineken (made in Holland and served onboard) to provide free beer. The brand recorded 800 bottles of Heineken consumed over the three days. Tied to this, a special happy hour giveaway featuring a travel package with round-trip airfare for two from JFK Airport in New York to Amsterdam, hotel accommodations, and tickets to Sensation. On the gastronomy end, KLM brought its onboard offerings to life with daily waffle happy hours featuring free Dutch coffee and stroopwafels by Eat.Dutch.Waffles.

To help amplify the campaign, KLM launched an Instagram contest activated on-site. By tagging posts with #KLMPOPUP, consumers had the chance to win free branded merchandise. Other giveaways included the "cycle miles contest," where consumers raced for 60 seconds on stationary bikes. Those who went the farthest distance won a pair of economy tickets, while second- and third-place winners scored air miles.

Habit 5. User-Triggered Engagements

Design experiences that don't start until the target turns them on.

- *Short and Long.* Effective experiences offer self-triggered engagements of varying lengths.

- *High-Net-Worth Attendees.* Create different engagements for different audiences. Provide a more premium experience to customers more likely to buy than to those who aren't.
- *Carve a Path.* Use self-triggered interactives to guide targets through a space.
- *Unmanned Experiences.* Embrace technology and social media as the primary platforms for self-triggered interactives.

Example: In 1967, Canadian Club began hiding cases of its whisky in remote locations throughout the world and sponsoring hunts for the cases (some were never found). In 2010, the Hide A Case Hunt, one of the longest-running spirits experiential campaigns, came back—inviting consumers to help find one of those lost cases, missing for more than 40 years.

Puzzles and clues were solved online for the preliminary competition, which ran from May to July. Competitors of legal drinking age registered at hideacase.com, and each week they were challenged to solve a puzzle, which, if answered correctly, earned them 10 points and the right to proceed to the next round of competition. To get through the preliminary round, consumers had to rack up at least 50 points from the six weekly puzzles; those who did moved to round two. In the second stage, consumers created a video illustrating why they should be chosen to join the live expedition to find the case and have a shot at winning a $100,000 grand prize. In July, the 30 best videos went up online for popular voting and before a panel of judges in order to narrow the field down to four Americans and four Canadians. In the final showdown the following April, those eight adventurers headed off into the wild to compete against one another in a series of scavenger hunts and trivia challenges designed to reveal the location of one of the few remaining hidden cases of whisky.

Habit 4. Effect and Affect

Experiences that touch the heart impact the mind.

- *Get Real.* The human connection is undeniable. Using real stories, real people, and real emotions creates the ultimate authentic connection.

- *Serve a Purpose.* Marketing with meaning—connections to causes, community, and charities—serves as an experiential magnet.
- *Focus.* The most authentic experiences speak to a specific audience—not every audience.
- *Tell a Story.* Use experiences to tell a branded story that people will relate to, understand, and want to become a part of.

Examples: Advil's Relief in Action program wanted to establish Advil as the "go-to" name in pain relief, especially for the thousands of volunteers across America who work tirelessly to help those in need, even when they may be in pain themselves. The 28-week Mobile Relief Center tour made approximately 100 stops in 12 states, visiting national, regional, and community-focused events, as well as unplanned ones, distributing water, snacks, seating, shelter, and Advil pain reliever.

During national volunteer events, such as the Capitol Hill People's Fair, the tour drove awareness for the program and recruited new volunteers. At regional events, including Clean Ocean Action Beach Sweep, the brand concentrated on quality engagement with volunteers as well as recruitment. It also gave a boost to volunteers at the ongoing Hurricane Katrina relief and Habitat for Humanity New Orleans programs. Advil captured stories in the Volunteer Story Booth, then shared them on its Facebook page. Consumers also could take the Volunteer Pledge to show their commitment to volunteerism.

After 82 event days, the programs touched 86,513 consumers, delivered more than 70,000 samples, and captured 340 volunteer stories. Of those consumers engaged, more than 4,000 took the Volunteer Pledge. The brand garnered 3.7 million impressions, and 88 percent of consumers surveyed said they would likely use Advil in the future.

Elsewhere, Lowe's home-grown Home Safety Council charity used a mobile tour for many years to teach kids how to help parents make homes safe—and drive parents to stores to buy the purchases they'd need for safer homes.

Two sets of trucks staffed by four safety experts unfolded into 1,200-square-foot "houses" featuring true-to-life living spaces children explored for hands-on safety tips. The effort targeted kindergarten through fifth grade students. At each event, mascot Rover the Safety Hound greeted kids, then got them ready for a 40-minute adventure with an orientation video. Each child was then armed with a flashlight and taken through the house with one of four trained Safety Rangers leading them in pointing out danger zones in the home. Each room had a lesson. In the kitchen, for example, kids went through a "what's wrong with this picture?" exercise in which they were asked to point out hazards such as poisons under the sink and hot stoves. Other stops included Rover's bathroom, backyard, and bedroom.

As the youngsters learned how to identify the hazards (trips and falls, fire, strangulation, and suffocation), the dangers were corrected. The finale was a fire drill with simulated smoke the kids crawled through. The "field trip on wheels" made stops at four schools (maximum throughput is 600 kids per day) during the week before setting up at Lowe's stores on the weekend, prompting kids to bring Mom and Dad to the store to show off what they've learned. The parents could then go into the store and buy the necessary safety improvement items.

Each year, the two trucks visited 31 markets and touched 130,000 children. Overall awareness and popularity of the program increased substantially. Sales were also impacted, with 32 percent of parents admitting to making at least one major change in their home as a result of the Great Safety Adventure and 11 percent making "significant changes." Thirty percent of kids who go through the experience end up teaching parents or siblings how to reduce hazards.

Elsewhere, upscale dinner delivery service Plated put its meals on wheels for a nine-city mobile tour that brought its pre-portioned seasonal ingredients and original recipes to consumers across the country on a retrofitted 1970s-era Airstream trailer. The goal: bring the brand's mission of helping consumers cook more and live better to life with a premium multisensory experience. The solution: the Road to Discovery Tour.

At each stop of the nine-week program, Plated invited consumers to take a journey through the brand's core pillars: source, curate, and deliver. After climbing aboard the Airstream, which was fully customized to reflect a modern home kitchen, visitors participated in a series of engagements designed to help them discover new ingredients, recipes, and cooking techniques.

To begin the experience, attendees explored an installation of living herbs located on the exterior of the trailer. They were then directed to a recipe stand outside the door to the Airstream, where they could choose their favorite Plated recipe from a collection of six recipe cards.

Next, guests were welcomed into the vehicle and asked to take a personal flavor profile quiz on an iPad. Participants then received a recommended herb blend that matched their flavor profile, along with a sample of the blend in a branded spice jar. As an added bonus, those who took the quiz were automatically entered into a sweepstake to win a free one-month Plated subscription.

Participants were then encouraged to explore the rest of the Airstream's interior, where they could engage with spices displayed on a custom table, learn how Plated meals and ingredients are delivered, and acquire cooking tips via a flat-screen TV. The tour also included daily cooking demonstrations led by Plated's culinary team, which used a mix of the brand's recipes. In addition to the Plated demos, several tour stops featured guest chefs from local restaurants who provided step-by-step preparation techniques. More than 16,000 consumers boarded the Airstream and, with the help of a microsite, social impressions totaled 4.8 million.

Elsewhere, to bring the stylish and customizable elements of its devices to life and to pilot a new retail strategy, Motorola opened Moto Shop, a pop-up store in downtown Chicago. The Moto Shop, with its customization theme that maps back to the brand's MotoMaker.com website, ran for three months.

The shop featured eight zones that offered tactile experiences and one-on-one conversations with product specialists. Among them, the Moto Maker Design Zone, which brought MotoMaker.com to life. Consumers could check out the website on Lenovo tablets and build physical inspiration boards on 12-inch branded trays (featuring the #xomotox tag) using different accessories and textures. The table showcased all of the different device backings on offer, from wood to leather. In the Moto 360 Zone, consumers could interact with the brand's smart watches, test out features, and browse in a jewelry store style environment.

In the Droid Turbo 2 Drop Zone, consumers could put the Shatter-Shield technology to the test, dropping the device onto a Bounce Zone complete with four surfaces—asphalt, hardwood, tile, and concrete. Footage displayed on an adjacent 90-inch monitor compared the Droid Turbo 2 and its shield to competitors' products. Consumers could also test out camera features with props and two backdrops to choose from (white or scenery), and then share their photos on social media for the chance to win prizes.

Finally, at a Choice Café, consumers sat at the counter and ordered from baristas. Orders were processed via text, displayed on Moto 360 devices that the baristas wore. In the process, consumers could have one-on-ones with product specialists while waiting or enjoying their java. Behind the counter, a monitor displayed a social feed of the photos tagged and posted from the activation.

"When we look at the young Millennial and Gen Z consumer—they define themselves by what they do, not what they have, and so I really believe it's important for brands to connect with those generations of consumers who don't covet the device themselves—they covet what they can produce with it. That was really the essence of the philosophy when looking at bringing the experience to life within the shop," Ketrina Dunagan, Motorola's vice president of global brand and marketing communications, told us.

Habit 3. Personalized

No two people should have the same experience.

- *Different Engagements.* Design the experience so attendees can engage in different ways, in different orders, and for different lengths of time.
- *Watch It.* Learn from the traffic, the behavior, and the ways targets interact.
- *Real-Time Transactions.* There's no better place to let people purchase than at a live experience.
- *Embrace Digital Wallets.* The emergence of digital payment platforms and currency is providing brands with the ability to sell product at their experiences.

Example: To attract tech-minded Millennial youths and young adults, the Air Force Recruiting Service launched the Air Force Performance Lab, one of its most personalized experiential tours ever. As discussed in Chapter 4, the program was designed to highlight career opportunities, the Lab visited air shows, schools, and other events.

Hyper-personalization began at registration with RFID wristbands that captured attendee data and tracked and computed their scores throughout the five interactives on-site. The Air Force was able to assess qualified leads through its digital data capture program, and from there, recruiters were able to connect with attendees in real time and answer any questions they might have about the Air Force or a specific career field.

Once inside the Lab, housed in a bump-out 18-wheeler trailer, attendees competed with each other via a series of challenges and interactive games that tested spatial and mechanical skills, dexterity, situational awareness, logic and reasoning, and physical strength. The experience began with high-tech puzzles offered on touch-screen monitors and equipped with two-minute quizzes.

From there, guests moved to the Oculus Rift activation, which represented the largest mixed use of technology in an Air Force recruiting experience—combining Kinect 2 motion sensory tech and Oculus Rift VR. Attendees were strapped into a cockpit setting equipped with rumble packs to mimic the vibrations of a jet, a joystick, and then the Oculus headset. The 360-degree skills-blind course lasted several minutes and had consumers flying an F-35 and following a wingman through a canyon. The goal was to navigate through graphical rings and be as accurate as possible.

Outside the mobile trailer, attendees took part in a Kinect 2–based physical challenge during which they chose a Special Ops airman or airwoman and competed against him or her, virtually, to see how many pull-ups they could do in 30 seconds. All throughout the experience, the consumers' individual scores were displayed on a leaderboard. The final experience was an interactive career center featuring a wall of 30 removable iPads that each displayed information on an Air Force career. The center helped the Air Force reinforce the marketing message that its branch of the armed services offers more than 150 careers.

Habit 2. Experiences Are Content

Brand experiences have become marketers' leading content capture tool and content distribution platform.

- *Content Factory.* Treat the experience as a primary channel for sourcing content for the entire marketing mix.

- *Self-Generation.* Design an engagement that stimulates an audience to capture and share content to their social circles.
- *Study the Brand.* There's no better living focus group and market research study than the one taking place at a live experience.
- *Power Users.* Fill audiences with targets who are not only relevant for the brand but are also heavy content sharers serve up a win-win.

Example: Wanting to get its technology into the hands of young-minded consumers, Samsung tapped into their love of music and film—and the rise of the 15-second video. The brand brought its Galaxy S6 and S6 Edge mobile phones, with their powerful camera capabilities and fast-charging functionality, to summer music festivals where attendees used the devices to capture video and photo content to share on social media.

Prior to each music fest, attendees received RFID wristbands that they registered online with their personal information. On-site, they scanned the wristband with NFC technology onto Samsung Galaxy phones to capture photos and video that were automatically posted to a personalized landing page, along with exclusive content created in partnership with a band at each festival. A follow-up e-mail drove users to their landing page with links to share the content on Facebook and Twitter. By sharing the content, consumers were entered to win tickets for weekend performances at the festival.

Three Samsung footprints at each festival featured a five-screen ultra-high-definition Samsung TV, wall-mounted on a truss that displayed the festival schedule, consumer-created content, tips for using the S6, and a social aggregator of consumers posting to #NEXTISNOW.

Habit 1. Bold, No-Fear Ideas

Nothing impacts the success of the experience like a fresh, creative idea.

- *Exert Strength.* If you want to be a leader in experiential marketing, act like it. Be bold and do what others haven't done.
- *Have Faith in Relevance.* The best campaigns are the ones with the most original ideas *and* the most relevant experiences.

- *Episodic Planning.* Effective experiential marketing programs are developed not as one-offs but more as episodes in a long-term strategy. Design campaigns that can live on for months, even years.
- *Test and Gamble.* Big ideas often come from gut instincts, rather than focus groups. Don't be afraid to gamble on a big hunch or test a huge idea.

Example: Friskies leveraged a feline competition between social media "celebri-cats" Grumpy Cat and Nala Cat to promote its catfood products. The Friskies Create & Taste Kitchen, located in a tricked-out space in New York, offered fans meet-and-greets and games, and raised awareness and donations for local shelter cats.

Here's how it worked: Each cat represented a hashtag and Friskies product. Consumers were encouraged to post about which "team" they were on—along with that team's hashtag. Leading #TeamSaucy and Friskies SauceSations canned food was "notorious curmudgeon" Grumpy Cat. Leading #TeamTender was "sweet" Nala Cat representing the Friskies Grillers with Meaty Tenders dry food.

Consumers could take selfies with the cats (perched on pedestals that looked like stacked catfood cans) during set times throughout the day-long event. Cat lover and WWE Diva Natalya also made appearances. There were games such as branded Plinko and a prize search in a ball pit, the results from which triggered donations of Friskies meals to shelters. Brand ambassadors kept track of wins associated with each game and "team" on a scoreboard.

As an added bonus, there was an ice cream station featuring "tender," "crunchy," or "saucy" toppings. In addition, Friskies partnered with PetFinder to showcase adoptable shelter cats in the Friskies Create & Taste Kitchen. The cats were located in a quiet corner of the event space alongside a gallery of their names and descriptions.

Consumers unable to attend the event could still help shelter cats by sharing whether their cat was on #TeamSaucy or #TeamTender. Every use of the hashtags on Twitter and Instagram triggered a donation—up to 10,000 meals. To build buzz for the event, Friskies offered a two-day preview of the space; passersby could get a glimpse into the kitchen through peepholes in the storefront window signage (including a peek at the shelter cats playing and resting in their housing pod). A virtual Friskies Create & Taste Kitchen experience was offered at friskies.com/ friskieskitchen.

EMBRACING EXPERIENTIAL

Don't equate great campaigns with big budgets. While we love to throw around the big-budget case studies, we've seen incredible experiences created with shoestring budgets.

And despite the core strategies and 10 habits presented, we find that at the heart of the best campaigns are bold yet simple ideas, a relevant yet exciting story, and a well-defined audience that is happy to exchange engagement for the right experiences.

Chapter Nine   The Vocabulary of Experiences

As marketers continue the transition to experiential marketing, they are witnessing first-hand how a completely different approach can drive incredible engagement and ROI. In broad strokes, the transition represents six fundamental changes in how companies market:

- *New Direction.* Companies are switching from marketing used to *push* customers toward their products and instead are using engagements that *pull* them.
- *Better Touchpoints.* Companies have replaced marketing campaigns designed to simply reach as many people as possible (quantity) with initiatives that seek to create longer conversations and deeper recall (quality) with the "right" people.
- *Authentic Engagements.* Marketers are no longer buying mere *impressions* and instead are investing in creating *expressions*.
- *Deeper Interactions.* Brands are transitioning from campaigns used to grab attention to programs created to give it.
- *Real Conversations.* Companies are no longer just talking to their customers—they are now focused on listening to them.

- *Lifelong Relationships.* Marketers are no longer trying to communicate their products' benefits to customers, but instead are using marketing to build relationships.

Embracing those six fundamental changes requires an experiential marketing learning curve featuring new features, functions, and terms. We've listed more than three dozen of them to get you on the track to talking the experiential talk.

NEW MARKETING FEATURES, FUNCTIONS, AND TERMS

Ambient Commerce

Integrating point-of-sale opportunities into live experiences. Based on the premise that engaged participants are more likely to buy as a result of an experience—so marketers should give them opportunities to make a purchase *during* an experience.

Auto-Sharing

The evolution of the share path carved from live experience to social media. First came social media kiosks, allowing event attendees at both consumer and business-to-business events to post information about their experience online. Today marketers are using technology such as RFID and interactives driven by Kinect platforms and mobile apps to "auto-tag" where a person is and what he or she is doing—then auto-post their photos, videos, and content to that person's social media platforms.

Example: Coca-Cola activated a summer program in Israel that users registered for from their Facebook accounts—and included a webcam scan of their faces—to gain entry. Facial recognition kiosks throughout the events captured photos, activities, location, and more; all were instantly posted to that person's social media pages. Each event hosted 650 consumers a day, and with the seamless Facebook integration, generated in excess of 35,000 posts each day of the three-day event (see page 101 for more details on this campaign).

Capacity Halos

Using the appearance of a sold-out event to drive heightened levels of desirability among target audiences—and faster levels of registration. Creating the perception that the event is about to "sell out" often motivates audiences to want to attend.

Cause-and-Effect Experiences

Tying into an existing experience that involves a specific and apparent problem that a brand can solve.

Example: Mondelēz International's Halls cough drop brand used sponsorship of the Association of Volleyball Professionals (AVP) to launch a new Halls Fruit Breezers line extension. The product, marketed as the solution for "dry, scratchy throats," was handed out at volleyball tournaments that take place near salt water and sand—hence an entire audience with dry, scratchy throats in need of a fix.

Content-Driven Experiences

Marketers are becoming much more focused on using content—creating it, amplifying it, and distributing it. In many cases, the actual experience is now designed and used specifically to generate content for the rest of the marketing mix. And attendees themselves are being used as both content creators and content amplifiers. Bud Light's first Whatever, USA program used 1,000 attendees to generate 37,000 pieces of content viewed by 15 million people. Numbers like that give marketers the power to reach more people than advertising with experiences. Bud Light VP Alex Lambrecht told us "the event has become a content factory." (For a deeper look at this program, see page 44.)

Cost Per Touch

This is the standard cost benchmark in experiential marketing. Typically generated by dividing the total budget by the total number of people reached.

Crowdsourcing

When groups of people make decisions for companies or brands. Companies are allowing their customers to have a voice in advertising messaging, outdoor billboard placement, even product development. At a time when marketers are crowing about "relevant experiences," crowdsourcing guarantees relevancy, as a target audience molds and shapes the marketing.

Examples: Oracle's event department used the power of crowdsourcing when it went beyond soliciting simple feedback from past OpenWorld attendees—and literally turned over session planning to 40,000 members of its Mix social media platform. Within weeks, more than 400 session topics were submitted, as well as other suggestions that streamlined the event. Elsewhere, So Delicious, a dairy-free brand, incorporated a digital component in its 27-market, bicoastal summer mobile tour, allowing consumers along tour routes to tweet a request for sampling teams to visit them at places such as their office, gym, or local park. The tweets were populated on a "tweet wall" on the tour microsite, which showed where sampling teams were located and what consumers were tweeting, live.

Digital Feeders

Using social media platforms and websites to drive live attendance to events. Often an invite to join an experience is only available online—a strategy used specifically to drive online to offline engagement.

Digital Resistance

Planning experiences with an understanding of how much digital engagement an audience wants and will accept. No two audiences have the same digital resistance.

Experience Gates

Requiring a "behavioral transfer" of some sort to take place between target and brand in order for the experience to begin. Social media gates make sharing on social platforms a requisite part of participation. Data gates require the transfer of information to take place prior to an experience. Trial gates require that someone partake in a product demo to gain admittance to an experience.

Experiential Temperature

Creating an experience that connects the brand and the target requires the right "experience temperature." At Target, for example, live experiences are designed to be varying levels of "cool" (hip, exclusive, sleek) or "hot" (sexy, exciting, heart-pumping). That temperature can be raised or lowered depending on the goal, strategy, and event, Target VP-experiential marketing Dan Griffis told us.

Experience Streams

The third and fourth screens have arrived as marketers tap into streaming—broadcasting live experiences via the web, devices, or via person-to-person platforms such as Meerkat, as well as from different points across a single event. Most business-to-business experiences have moved fast to stream content and activities from trade shows, conferences, and proprietary events, but consumer marketers are activating live streams as well.

Examples: Salesforce's Dreamforce amplifies its experience using full-time live broadcasts. Target's sponsorship of the Grammy Awards was brought to life via a live Imagine Dragons broadcast that served as a streamable event and as the first-ever live-broadcast TV commercial.

Fear of Missing Out (FOMO)

FOMO taps into the emotional anxiety over missing out on something important. Marketing campaigns are using the fear of missing out on an experience as an element of motivating a target to want to be a part of it. Smirnoff for years used its "Be There" platform, and activated FOMO-inducing "you had to be there" experiences.

Forced Trial

Creating experiences that either require a product trial or design participation around a product trial. No other form of marketing can stimulate and/or facilitate a live use of a product or service.

Fused Experiences

Events used to engage new customers and bolster relationships with existing customers—at the same time.

Example: To drive new users, re-engage lapsed customers, and increase current customer usage, eBay used a series of Camp eBay events designed to engage two targets using a custom mobile camp cabin and custom school bus. The cabin was used as an eBay 101 for new users, the bus as an eBay 301 for existing users.

Gamification

Integrating elements of game playing (point scoring, competition with others, rules of play) into a brand experience. Allows marketers to talk to an audience less and play with an audience more. Studies show that when an audience enjoys an experience, memorability and inclination to buy rise.

High-Net-Worth Targets

Using experiences to engage subsections of an audience that have a high value to a brand—either because of current or prospective spending level or other non-monetary beneficial influence.

Hub-and-Spoke Events

The combination of large "hub" events with localized "spoke" events. The hubs draw larger numbers of attendees while the spokes appeal to target audiences who might not be able to travel and attend.

Example: Cisco's GSX conference used three hub conferences tethered to almost 100 spoke events. The program delivered online connections as well as face-to-face experiences to 21,000 attendees from the hub-and-spoke model, which Cisco said at the time set a new standard for how large organizations communicate messages via experiences.

Hypertargeting

Experiences can be used to target very specific audiences that brands can't reach using traditional marketing. An ad campaign may allow brands to reach moms, but an experiential marketing program can be used to reach single moms who like yoga and eat gluten-free foods.

Incubator Experiences

These take place within existing experiences and typically involve sub-sections of attendees meeting with other attendees to discuss a problem, come up with an idea, or work with the brand to create or generate content.

Example: AT&T brings nearly 700 top developers together each year to its Developer Summit Conference to show off what it's been working on for the past year, then see what the community thinks of its products and innovations. But the real draw is a hackathon. AT&T offered $100,000 in cash and prizes across several categories, designed to encourage collaboration, learning, and innovative application development. The focus: "The Internet of Things," or the connected car, connected home, and wearable tech. Participants had two days to build and code a mobile app solution with help from several key sponsors and AT&T partners, in addition to input from the three hackathon mentors. The top three teams pitched their apps to attendees during the conference keynote for the chance to win the grand prize.

Living Attributes

Designing a physical experience based on the attributes or physical appearance of a brand or product allows a marketer to take an audience "inside the brand."

Example: To celebrate Whirlpool's 15th anniversary in Europe for 1,500 dealers and employees, the company produced a multi-day event that invited guests to "experience the vision" of Whirlpool Europe. Lectures and general sessions were presented on a rotating auditorium designed to feel like a Whirlpool washing drum. The Immersion Zone, as it was called, was surrounded by multiple stage sets. Rotating the attendees delivered 10 different interactions in a single space.

Loaner Experiences

Putting your product into the hands of potential customers and encouraging them to use it in their own environment.

Example: To drive awareness and trial of its new Chromebook, Google designed a lending program through experiential partnerships with Virgin

America airlines and the Ace Hotel in New York City. Chromebook is a personal computer that runs on Google's Chrome OS operating system. Since the product was initially only available online, the lending program offered consumers a chance to experience the product for an extended time, while they were in the air or in their hotel rooms using a free Wi-Fi connection. Travelers flying on Virgin America between San Francisco and Boston, Chicago O'Hare, or Dallas could borrow a Chromebook to use in-flight, then return it when they landed. Ace Hotel guests found a Chromebook attractively packaged in felt-like holders and placed on their beds when they entered their rooms. The Chromebook was loaded with an app created with the hotel, which informed users of things to do and places to visit while they were in town.

Participatory Experiences

Using ongoing participation to drive an experience. Target audiences and brands maintain communication and contact to keep the experience going.

Example: Heineken's Star Player campaign was anchored by a second-screen gaming experience that European soccer fans could engage while watching matches on TV. A Star Player app allowed viewers of UEFA Champions League games to interact with the action in real time, syncing with the game clock when the match began. Users could then earn points by predicting game events such as goals and corner kick outcomes, and by answering questions during periodic pop-up quizzes. Players competed against friends in a mini-league and could also check their rank against all the app users.

Pop-Ups

Temporary experiences traditionally set up for days or weeks. The term is most often connected to pop-up stores, which are branded experiences that take over vacant retail spaces—although pop-ups have also been executed in airports, on street corners, on college campuses, and at business-to-business events.

Queue Experiences

Creating deliberate interactions with the people waiting in lines to get into an experience.

Example: At the Winter Olympics, where long lines began forming early in the morning, Coca-Cola trained a team of "Happiness" ambassadors with the sole mission of keeping folks content as they waited in line to enter the Coke Pavilion. The ambassadors did everything from waves and high fives to cheering the campaign slogan "Open Happiness" in English and French. The design of the line is also important. (Coke's team laid out the queue so people could face the brand's Jumbotron airing Olympic competitions and updates.)

Random Experiences

Events that leverage surprise, delight, and crowdsourcing . . . and are not 100 percent planned or repeated.

Example: Kipling, a maker of handbags and accessories whose brand logo includes a long-tailed monkey and the words Make Happy, used brand ambassadors to "share happiness" by passing out free flowers, sweet treats, and pre-filled transit cards from pink branded trucks. Brand ambassadors also visited select offices in the city with surprises for employees nominated by co-workers to receive a Make Happy visit.

Replication Events

Translating TV spots into live events. Most often used for generating media attention for a new marketing campaign.

Example: To translate a new ad campaign for its Opel brand's Insignia model, breaking during the London Motor Show, General Motors crafted a highly produced stunt that unraveled a bit each day to keep the press and public in suspense and tuned in. Held at Potters Field Park with the iconic Tower Bridge looming in the background, the stunt played up Insignia's X-Files-themed ad campaign. GM planted an orb into the ground as if it had plunged to the earth from outer space. Scenic artists ensured the details around the orb seemed authentic to a crash site (sections of Styrofoam were painted to resemble dirt impaled by a smoking object). The next morning Londoners awoke to find the area cordoned off with "caution" signs and security guards dressed in black suits. The Insignia logo was discreetly placed on the exterior of the orb and on the lapels of pseudo-security guards' uniforms. GM wowed not only the automotive press, but also got on CNN lifestyle blogs and You-Tube, as it had planned.

Screened Interactions

The many ways target audiences engage a brand experience on a screen. Think screened shopping, screened education, screened conversations. Marketers must be conscious that people are engaging their experiences on a screen of some size and architect the engagements based on those platforms.

Sequence Journeys

Using deliberately designed paths to guide attendees through an experience. We've seen this also referred to as an "experience continuum" and "experience mapping." Very closely tied to the elements of experience design (for more on Experience Design, see Chapter 6), Journey Sequencing allows marketers to essentially put the target audience on a predefined and predesigned axis through a brand experience without the participants feeling as though they're being guided or directed.

Service Experiences

Offering target audiences a high-value service in exchange for an engagement.

Examples: Motorola set up shoe-shine stations in office parks. Consumers who wanted a free shoe shine were invited to take a seat and get one—and during the shine, brand ambassadors showed them some of the newest Motorola phones. Elsewhere, Procter & Gamble offered parents with small children complimentary car safety seat inspections in retail parking lots. While one brand ambassador was checking the car seat, another was telling the parents about the attributes of Pampers diapers.

Simultanevents

Market-by-market event schedules are being upgraded with campaigns running multiple events simultaneously. It's all part of an effort by marketers to speed up reach, frequency, and go-to-market timelines.

Examples: MetLife's Day One, a program connecting current employees and those of newly acquired Alico, spawned 60 events that touched 70,000 employees in 64 countries. To generate awareness and drive demos of its new Eikon desktop software, Thomson Reuters staged Go Live events in 14 cities at the same time. Video street teams broadened the effort, recording financial professionals' thoughts on what they would like to see more or less of in the industry. The videos ran on LED boxes in London and New York City. The campaign included a street-level art installation and a competition to win a trip to the South Pole.

Social Attendance

Using social media to build the actual attendance for experiences. From Facebook and Twitter to YouTube and the like, social media has officially become a legitimate *feeder* for live events.

Example: Bacardi's Like It Live campaign allowed consumers who "like" the brand on Facebook to vote on what elements, activities, and design aspects actually made up the campaign's events taking place around the country. Not only did consumers control the look and feel of the events, but *all* event attendance came from those who interacted with Bacardi on Facebook.

Social Currency

Exchanging an experience for a specific social media activity.

Examples: When Kellogg's opened a Tweet Shop in London to promote the launch of its Cracker Crisps, the brand "charged" consumers tweets for free samples. Elsewhere, Pepsi rolled out Like Machines, vending machines that charged a Facebook "like" for a soda. (Consumers logged into their accounts and liked the soda brand from the vending machine's touch screen front.)

Social Listening

Using social media channels to monitor, learn, and listen to customers. Listening is less about a dialog and much more about keeping a watchful eye on audiences and learning from them.

Example: At Cisco's annual Cisco Live event, the company creates an actual Social Media Command Center staffed by five Cisco employees responsible for monitoring ongoing topics, trending, and sentiment across social platforms.

Storydoing

The age of storytelling is getting an upgrade as marketers use experiences to not just *tell* a story, but create a story in which attendees "do" that story—by participating in the narrative and living it for a moment or moments in time. Storydoing is a philosophy being embraced by Fortune 500 experiential departments: Attendees become a part of the event and actually drive the experience themselves via highly interactive footprints, shareable engagements, and customized event activities.

The Village Format

The physical footprint of business-to-business experiences—which long used breakout rooms, general sessions, and trade show exhibit areas—has been recast as marketers use fewer, but larger, more singular experiences that house all content and activities in one space.

Transactional Experiences

Leveraging transactional experiences that allow target audiences to buy or place orders for products *on-site*. Trade shows and business-to-business events are taking deposits for product from interested buyers, a move that increases the chance of obtaining a complete purchase over the traditional act of simply collecting a lead. And business-to-consumer events, long relegated to pushing consumers to the nearest store, are now selling everything from cases of soda and cell phones, to laptops and cars on-site using tablets, credit-card swipers, and kiosks.

Example: When Smart USA launched its tiny ForTwo vehicle, the company wanted to cut the amount of typical "lag" time between an event test-drive and follow-up from a local dealer. The company took $99 deposits from drivers, a small token to consumers but a large indication of purchase intent. Smart fast-tracked those leads (20,000 in the first six months) directly to dealers same-day.

Unmanned Experiences

Oculus Rift chairs, social walls, gesture media, and event wearables. Motion detection, location detection, engagement detection. Companies are replacing brand ambassadors and embracing "the machine" as their latest interactive channel. These experiences are designed around attendee-triggered interactives and anchored by *unmanned* technologies that attendees start and end on their own.

Zoned Experiences

Engagements designed around "zoned" footprints, each of which provides different messages and interactives. Often, zoned programs use fun and excitement in the initial zones, and sales offers in the final ones.

Example: The New York Times used a five-zone experience within its exhibit at the annual South by Southwest event. The first few zones allowed attendees to take videos and create customer flipbooks—and the final zone offered a discounted subscription.

Chapter Ten   Converting to an Experience Brand

Congratulations. You've made it this far—and if you're ready to commit to adopting an experiential strategy for your company or your brand, then some important, and potentially uncomfortable, decisions lie ahead. For it's not enough to understand the theories and mimic some of the great campaign examples you've read about. In order to reap the rewards of experiential marketing—stronger relationships, better marketing ROI, and increased business impact—then you must prepare your organization to embrace the strategy by taking seven very specific steps.

STEP 1. IDENTIFY YOUR FRONTS

The first step is to narrow your marketing focus around the key "fronts" that you will use as platforms from which to build partnerships and programs. Your fronts should align your brand with the interests, passions, and demographics of your customers. For a luxury auto brand like Lexus, for example, their fronts are Affluent Sports, Eco-Luxury Living, Enthusiasts, and Epicurean, and it's around these fronts that the company concentrates its experiential efforts by seeking established events like food and wine festivals that are *relevant* to their customer base, where they can create a *significant presence*, and where that presence is *authentic to the brand*.

But in order to be truly experiential, your brand cannot just "be there." Your presence must improve the event, improve perception of the event, and improve the perception of your brand or company by its presence at the event. When Asics signed on as a sponsor of the New York Marathon, the company went beyond banners and logoed merchandise and created a program that accomplished all three improvement goals. Knowing that marathon running is a solitary sport that requires many months of time and training, the company worked with the New York Road Runners Club to provide personalized supporter messages that loved ones could send to their runners during the race. The pre-recorded videos and text messages were displayed on massive LED screens and were triggered by RFID tags as runners crossed over special sensor mats placed throughout the course. Runners could be seen weeping with pride as their loved ones popped up on giant screens to urge them on. The program was so impactful that other marathon organizers reached out to Asics to bring the program to their races.

STEP 2. FIND AND ALIGN PARTNERS

Once you've identified your fronts, it's time to evaluate and select the partner properties you will work with to create and execute your experiential programs.

If you will be investing in sponsorship of existing events, be sure to negotiate how you can leverage your participation to gain access to the property's assets in a way that creates a win-win scenario. Your goal should be to go beyond buying just space or logo placement. BMW, for example, used its partnership with the U.S. Olympic Committee to connect with existing owners of its vehicles by tying a summer test-drive program to its all-new 6 Series, as well as its partnership with the U.S. Olympic Committee. The company created an integrated marketing campaign that included print and web invites and a promotional kit that enabled local BMW centers to invite their customers to their driving events. Invitations included an incentive for the customers to participate: for each driver who attended the events, BMW donated $10 to Team USA in that person's name. When the drive was over, a former, current, or hopeful USA Olympian was present to speak with guests and talk about how important the partnership is between BMW and the U.S.O.C. Olympians like Shannon Miller, Olympic gold medalist in gymnastics, posed with the customers for photos and signed their commemorative BMW hats.

Customers were then asked to fill out a post-drive survey and were directed to a client advisor who offered them $1,000 off the purchase of a vehicle. A few weeks after the event, customers received a personal phone call from an Olympian thanking them for their purchase and their donations to Team USA. BMW engaged more than 20,000 consumers, which resulted in a 22 percent conversion rate of new BMW purchases within six months. In addition to an increase in brand awareness and sales, the events also brought to life BMW and Team USA's Olympics partnership during a non-Olympic year.

STEP 3. SELECT THE RIGHT AGENCY

Because experiential marketing has many moving parts, it's likely that you will work with several agency partners to create and execute some or all of your program elements. You might have an ad agency creating brand strategy and awareness campaigns; a PR firm handling publicity; a digital agency managing your social media strategy; an event agency handling event production and logistics; or you might have fewer agencies that are providing a wider array of services. As experiential marketing has exploded over the past few years, many large agency networks have acquired event and experiential marketing firms to beef up their full-service credentials. At the same time, new firms have sprouted, in many cases formed by those who split from acquired companies in order to offer experiential services independent of larger agency networks.

Your particular circumstances will dictate which type of agency (or mix of agencies) is right for your organization, but we offer this word of caution: experiential marketing is marketing without a net. The complex logistical nature of experiential marketing requires that those you entrust to represent you know what they are doing. Experiential programs are often high-profile endeavors that can be impacted by weather, scheduling issues, permit snafus, talent and staffing meltdowns, and myriad other "things that can go bump." Sadly, there is no college major in experiential marketing (although we're working on that!), so experience is gained by having done it. Be sure that during your agency evaluation process you ask for case studies and other evidence that your agencies have a solid track record of success. Experienced agencies will wow you with great ideas and flawless execution, but just as importantly, they will minimize the risks associated with this strategy.

STEP 4. FIX YOUR RFP PROCESS

One of the biggest areas where we see companies potentially missing out on the benefits of experiential marketing is the agency RFP process. It's ironic that a company's first step on its experiential journey is often the wrong step. This happens when a company uses an RFP designed for another type of agency engagement to hire an experiential firm. Other than the term "agency," there are few similarities between these specialized firms and others.

In fact, this issue has been so contentious that Geometry Global, a leading experiential firm that is part of the Ogilvy network, commissioned the Event Marketing Institute to study the RFP process. Our research found that, alongside the growth in the number of RFPs being issued to experiential agencies, comes an increased sense of frustration among many on both sides of the process. Underlying the frustration is when a process that is used to purchase commodities is used to screen and select companies that provide creative services and intellectual property. A key characteristic of an effective RFP process is the ability to best align a marketer's needs and goals with agency capabilities.

Our research found that brand marketers feel that their experiential RFP processes are "effective" to "moderately effective." But only 6 percent say their process is "very effective." Three out of four marketers (76 percent) say that their primary RFP-related challenge is the overall time commitment required to create, issue, and review RFPs. Forty-one percent of marketers also say that lack of staff with RFP experience, along with corporate policies that complicate the process, are key challenges (see Figure 10.2).

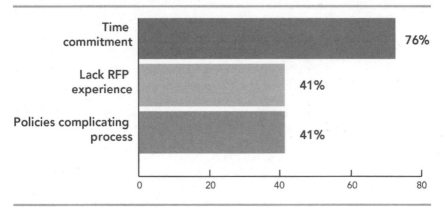

FIGURE 10.1   RFP Obstacles
Source: Geometry Global/EMI 2013 RFP Benchmark Study

RFP Obstacles

A key finding of the study is that more brands are issuing more RFPs. In fact, 74 percent of brands are issuing more or the same number of marketing RFPs compared to three years ago. This increase can be attributed to event marketing industry growth along with new event and experiential strategies and opportunities—social media, RFID, virtual events, and other initiatives—that marketers are seeking via RFPs. This trend also reflects the expansion of corporate procurement issues and practices, including cost and supplier management, into the marketing realm. But while corporate procurement may be driving the RFP process, it's the marketing department or a centralized corporate event marketing team that owns it and wields the most influence on the process (Figure 10.2).

Departments Involved in the Agency RFP Process

The study identified the components of successful RFPs by asking issuers and respondents what should be included and what was lacking. According to marketers, the most important elements of RFPs are clear and detailed explanations of their goals and objectives, as well as clear project requirements. When asked about agency RFP responses, marketers look for evidence that the agency clearly understands the marketer's industry or product category and their unique business and marketing needs and challenges. Additionally, agencies can help themselves by

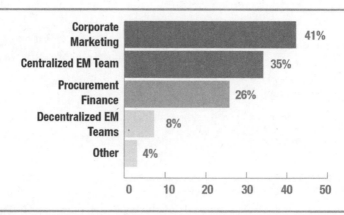

FIGURE 10.2   Departments Involved in the Agency RFP Process
Source: Geometry Global/EMI 2013 RFP Benchmark Study

asking detailed questions and providing more information on pricing and cost/value explanations.

Agency executives say that RFPs fall short when they lack sufficient details and direction or provide no or unrealistic budget parameters. In addition, lack of client access for questioning during the RFP process hinders their ability to respond effectively. Agency respondents felt that marketers and procurement teams have only a moderate level of understanding of cost structures for event-related purchases. More than half of agencies said that procurement groups have little to no understanding of industry cost structures. Interestingly, it may be this very statistic that is driving the use of RFPs, since pricing can vary widely from company to company, and events are unlike commodity products that have little differentiation beyond price. Event and experiential programs are based on ideas that often require complex executional and logistical coordination to be successful. For many marketers and their procurement departments, the RFP process is being used as a way to both screen partners as well as gain visibility on costs for a practice that does not have rate cards.

Agencies expressed more frustration with the RFP process than their brand counterparts, but both sides acknowledged more can be done to improve the process so that both buyer and seller can feel that the investment of time and resources in issuing and responding to RFPs is worth the effort. Among the recommendations for agencies were: (1) better understanding the client's industry/category, (2) taking time to study unique business needs, (3) asking more detailed questions during the process, and (4) providing more clarity on pricing. Recommendations for marketers include: (1) providing clear goals and objectives, (2) more information on past or current programs and results, (3) more background information, and (4) more time to develop responses.

STEP 5. BEEF UP YOUR INTERNAL TEAMS

As important as your external agency roster is your internal marketing team. It's important that you have an internal champion (or champions) who are aligned around your marketing objectives and who have access to, and the support of, top management, as well as the authority to make decisions. Too often we see internal experiential executives who feel that they are seen as "corporate wedding planners" and not strategic marketers. As experiential marketing has evolved from a tactic rooted in live event production to a strategy that uses live events as a platform with which to build relationships and create sustained business impact, you must ensure that the skillsets of your internal teams are where they need to be in order to manage your external partners, manage internal expectations, and deliver business value.

It will be the responsibility of your internal champions to manage your external partners and enforce discipline and alignment around your experiential goals. Internal and external turf battles are one of the biggest obstacles to experiential marketing success, and too often we have seen otherwise great promise undermined due to misaligned interests, motivations, and even compensation structures.

STEP 6. CREATE VALUE

Your goal should be not just to create value, but to create *meaningful* value for your company and your customers. By now you know that this is accomplished by creating programs that foster interactions that enrich consumer experiences in relevant ways. Successful experiential marketers check themselves at every touch point to ensure that each component of a program delivers an enhanced customer experience. Remember, experiential marketing is a journey, and for people to join you they have to see and feel that they are deriving value from their investment in time. It's your responsibility to think through each program from start to finish in order to ensure that you are providing value at every turn.

STEP 7. IMPROVE LOWER-FUNNEL RESULTS

While experiential marketing can impact the entire purchase funnel, it's critical that you focus on your lower-funnel results. This is where you will link participation to business impact. It's arguably the most important area to plan for, and the planning should begin at the outset of your campaign development. As an example, a company might sponsor a sporting event and create visibility with naming rights or branding around the event. This would provide the brand awareness at the upper end of the purchase funnel. The brand activation at the sporting event—athlete meet-and-greets, sampling activities, games, and so on—create customer engagement that impacts the middle of the funnel, where consumers gain product knowledge and brand affinity, and where advocacy is created.

The lower funnel is where you facilitate and document conversions. This is where you create a link between participation and action. Did they buy, and if so, how quickly? Did they become advocates for your brand? The key to reporting on these and other lower-funnel metrics is to build in your conversion strategy at the outset. If you want to track purchases, for example, you'll need a data-collection strategy to know who you engaged with, and a re-contact strategy to gauge purchases or at least purchase intent. In this example, you would need to design your engagement strategy to provide an experience (or an offer) that the participant sees as worth giving up his or her personal information.

Smart experiential marketers are continually building their lower funnels by integrating more and better online and on-site touch points to boost lead generation and drive consideration and purchase intent. As covered in Chapter 7: Proving Performance and Measurement, be sure you have internal buy-in to the lower-funnel metrics, and commit to a consistent measurement regimen that makes sense for your company.

If you're like us, you're fascinated and inspired by the creativity and business results that have been achieved by the scores of companies showcased in this book. But behind every successful campaign is a company that has embraced these seven steps to set the stage for what they were able to create and the business impact they were able to deliver. We hope that by now you are inspired to begin your own experiential journey. Believe it or not, if you can take the steps outlined here; then developing killer experiential campaigns will be relatively easy.

REFERENCE

Geometry Global/Event Marketing Institute. (2013). *2013 benchmark study*. New York: Geometry Global.

Acknowledgments

What you just read would not have been possible without the brands that inspired us, the friends who never stopped asking when we'd write a book, and the thousands of marketers who supported and encouraged us over the last 15 years.

Many thanks to our literary agent Matt Davis and his team at Wiley for their insight, enthusiasm, and acceptance of our dialing into conference calls from such random places as The Canyons in Park City, the Earl's Court stop on London's green line, Club Macanudo in New York City, and the Chili's by gate 34 at Tampa International Airport. Also to Don Pazour and our colleagues at Access Intelligence for their assistance and continued friendship (and employment), and to author Nick Tasler, whose advice during a late-night dash to the Lagos airport in Nigeria literally put this book in motion.

Special gratitude goes to the past and present editors of *Event Marketer* magazine—especially Jessica Heasley, Rachel Kirkpatrick,

Sandra O'Loughlin, and Kait Shea—for lending their voices and reporting skills to the case studies included throughout the book.

And finally, while we often refer to the experiential marketing industry as our family, a heartfelt thank you goes to our *actual* families who stick with us, put up with us, and love us despite the travel, the deadlines, and those continued trips to the Olympics, the Academy Awards, and the Super Bowl that really aren't as much fun as the photos make them look—*well, maybe they are.* XOXOXOX.

About the Authors

In 2002, Kerry Smith and Dan Hanover launched what would become the largest portfolio of experiential marketing content in the world—a global network that includes *Event Marketer* magazine, the Experiential Marketing Summit, The Ex Awards and the Event Marketing Institute. They are considered the world's foremost experts on experiential marketing—where it came from, how it's grown, why companies are using it, and what the future of the marketing mix looks like. They have trained hundreds of marketing teams across six continents at such companies as Procter & Gamble, Oracle, Mercedes, Cisco, Intel, Adidas, BMW, Pepsi, IBM, General Electric, AT&T, Kraft, Microsoft, McDonald's, Dell, Anheuser-Busch, 3M, Best Buy, Toyota, R.J. Reynolds, and many others.

Kerry Smith is a graduate of the S.I. Newhouse School of Public Communications at Syracuse University. Mr. Smith learned about the evolution of marketing from the inside out, first as an advertising agency executive in New York City and then as a media entrepreneur who launched a dozen marketing magazines and conferences over three decades. His company, Red 7 Media, was named one of fastest-growing privately held publishing companies in the United States by *Inc.* magazine in 2007 and 2008.

Dan Hanover is a graduate of the Harrington School of Communication and Media at the University of Rhode Island. Mr. Hanover has led award-winning content teams at some of the most respected media companies in the world. He is a recognized global authority on the advertising industry, promotion category, retail sector, licensing arena, entertainment category, and the experiential marketing industry. He is the founding editor-in-chief of *Event Marketer* magazine.

Contact them at infinitypartnersglobal.com.

Index

Page references followed by *fig* indicate an illustrated figure.